C Studies in Higher Education Fundraising

Critical Issues, Critical Discussions

By

G. David Gearhart
Professor, Higher Education. University of Arkansas

Michael T. Miller
Professor, Higher Education, University of Arkansas

NEW FORUMS

NEW FORUMS PRESS INC.

Published in the United States of America
by New Forums Press, Inc.1018 S. Lewis St.
Stillwater, OK 74074
www.newforums.com

Library of Congress Cataloging-in-Publication Data Pending

This book may be ordered in bulk quantities at discount from New
Forums Press, Inc., P.O. Box 876, Stillwater, OK 74076 [Federal
I.D. No. 73 1123239]. Printed in the United States of America.

ISBN 10: 1-58107-316-X
ISBN 13: 978-1-58107-316-4

Table of Contents

Case Studies by Fundraising Topic

The Lost Merger

Planned Gifts

Case Studies by Institutional Type

Foreword

In a world of uncertainties, particularly in higher education, one thing is certain: fundraising is vital to the operation, and even survival, of universities—private and public. Higher education leaders realize tuition revenue and legislative support alone will not build a great university, and only through private gift support can substantial endowments be built and scholarships provided for students, endowed faculty chairs and professorships created, and capital support to maintain bricks and mortar—not to mention the importance of annual giving which can provide unrestricted support for an institution. Private gift support is essential for any organization to advance in today's highly constrained resource environment.

At public universities, the decline of state support in recent years has been dramatic. Many major public research universities—highly prestigious ones—now receive less than 10% of their total support from the state tax dollar. Attempting to finance an institution "on the backs of students" through double-digit increases in tuition and "on the backs of faculty and staff" who may not receive even cost of living increases may ultimately be the demise of higher education. State government leaders must realize that continued cuts in higher education appropriations or, in the alternative, simply maintaining the status quo of an institution's budget, diminishes a state's economic and cultural future.

America has over one and a half million charitable nonprofit organizations, all of which are looking for private gift support. For many of these organizations, particularly arts organizations, human service agencies, and religious congregations, private contributions may be the sole source of their support. Such competition is now evident to all in the business of fundraising that philanthropy will continue to occupy a prominent role in all non-profit institutions, particularly colleges and universities. Giving has been a part of human life throughout recorded history and the United States has been characterized as the most charitable nation on earth, and this continues to be true in the 21st century as it was in the 18th, 19th and 20th centuries.

But, considerable change has occurred in fund raising over the last 20 to 30 years as the degree of involvement of donors has increased dramatically. Today, the donor, the benefactor, wants to be involved in how funds are being used at the philanthropy they are supporting. There is a feeling among Baby Boomer donors that they want their gift to have the biggest impact possible. Previous generations were not nearly as involved in gift use decision making. Today's donors need to understand and believe in what the organization is doing with their resources. Today, they want to see firsthand how their gifts will benefit society and the institution.

Related to the desire to understand and influence the use of their donations is the huge intergenerational transfer of trillions of dollars from the "greatest generation," those who grew up during the Great Depression and lived through World War II, to the Baby Boomers, those born between 1946 and 1964. These funds have made available enormous pockets of wealth and much of it is finding its way to eleemosynary organizations. Fundraising professionals have to be able to explain to these "new" donors how a donation will benefit programs and people.

On top of these changes is the coming of the electronic age of fundraising and the substantial use of social media. Most sophisticated annual fund campaigns today avail themselves of electronic fundraising in one form or another, or in multiple forms. Electronic solicitation delivery will continue to increase in use among most organizations seeking private gift support.

The result of all of these forces is the need to train and provide continuing education to the fundraising professional. Changes in tax law, creative ideas for working with benefactors, and strategic problem solving will all be critical to the development officer of the future.

Introduction

Case Studies in Action

The field of development or fundraising in higher education is changing rapidly, as an increasing number of non-profits and philanthropic entities are competing more aggressively for financial support. The number of non-profit organizations and 501(c)(3) entities has grown exponentially just in the last 10 years. Capital campaigns are at an all-time high and private gift support is a critical component of all non-profit organizations. Colleges and universities are particularly engaged in this aggressive competition, and as institutions use a more creative and a diverse range of program offerings and delivery strategies, their core relationships must be cultivated in different ways. College students are no longer traditionally-aged, residential learners, as online course offerings and executive programs provide students access to higher education in a very different way than a generation ago. As these different strategies deliver higher education to a broader population with greater and easier access, institutions also have less of a personal relationship with the student, leading to less allegiance toward a single alma mater. Similarly, the rapid growth of transferring credits from different institutions to patch-together a degree further diminish the single institution identity that has for so long been at the heart of higher education fundraising.

The case study teaching method is, by design, a strategy to engage students in an active learning process. Through the examination of different ideas being presented with changing 'facts,' and being confronted with hard questions, students are forced to take positions and defend them. This process of problem-solving, creating solutions, and taking sides forces students to confront biases, challenge each other, and ultimately, to come together around difficult situations.

The process of entering a dialogue with different ideas and perceptions of reality are very much what happens in the workplace, where differences are aired and vented in professional environments and where the actions of the group often carry tremendous consequences. Because of this, case study questions are answered best by groups of individuals who can share different thought processes on the topic or question at hand. Case study questions can, however, also be used to prompt individual reflection and can be effective tools to help the individual think about a topic, a situation, a setting, a problem differently. Ultimately, the goal of these case studies is to get individuals thinking differently about how to solve problems and to see issues from different perspectives; a critical skill necessary for the contemporary fundraising professional.

The facilitator of these case studies might find it helpful to try assigning groups or teams to respond to the cases, considering the strengths, backgrounds, and temperaments of the group. Conversely, random assignment of teams might result in very different responses and outcomes. By allowing individuals to self-select their groups, frequently the process will result in less controversy or critical questioning of each other. This grouping of individuals, whether students or fundraising professionals, should be done purposefully and with an understanding of what the intended outcome is for the experience.

Another strategy to aid in the use of case studies is to ask those responding to the questions to report to the larger group. With multiple small groups reporting to the entire larger group, questioning of responses by fellow participants can result in a deeper reflection and exploration of responses.

Depending on the time available for the use of the case studies, the facilitator may want to try timed responses, where groups have to come up with answers in a very short period of time. Alternating longer periods for discussion and consensus building among a group can be an effective strategy, especially when the facilitator can balance the use of short and long response periods. Allowing some groups to have a longer period for discussion and reflection, while other groups have to respond to questions as 'quick-hits,' can result in differing perceptions of problem solutions.

To further create discussion, the facilitator might also consider 'flipping' the responses, where some groups are asked to identify the counter-intuitive response. Some response might seem obvious as to what the best practice can or should be, and flipping the response outcome can result in a different level of critical questioning.

Whether used for team-building or in a classroom, these cases were designed and tested to prompt discussion, reflection, and consideration of different points of view.

All of the cases are based loosely on real-life events spanning over 65 years of experience in higher education. However, the actual cases are fictional, with fictional characters, institutions, time frames, and events to protect against abridgement of confidentiality.

The case method of study has been around since the time of Cicero and can be in contrast to other teaching methods. These cases do not have 'right' and 'wrong' answers or easy solutions. They present team members and students with an opportunity to explore multiple avenues under difficult circumstances. The use of role playing can also be an excellent tool to draw out opinions and attributes among group members. At the conclusion of the case study conversation, it is certainly appropriate for session leaders to offer opinions and other solutions based on personal and professional experiences. This can also be an excellent time to bring in expert panels and guest speakers who may have encountered similar challenges in their careers. However, caution is recommended that session leaders not give the impression that their solution is the only option. The cases in this book are complex and difficult, and team members and students will need plenty of questioning to absorb the complexities and nuances of each case.

Case Study 1:
Community College Donor Dilemma

Pine City is a major northwestern city of nearly 3 million people. Situated in a bowl surrounded by mountains, the city leaders taxed themselves in the early-1970s to create a community college, founding Western Community College, opening in 1976. The College began with a large number of vocational and occupational programs, but grew steadily throughout the 1980s and 1990s to reach a headcount enrollment of nearly 15,000 students. Although the full-time equivalency is less than a third of the enrollment, the College has prospered due largely to the growing tax base of the city and the additional support received directly from the state. Last fall the College reported offering 27 associate's degree programs and nearly 50 certificate and diploma programs. The College has also begun experimenting with online programs throughout the city and county.

Students joke about the campus parking situation, referring to the low-lying surface parking as "The Pit," but otherwise enjoy the modern physical plant and well-groomed campus. There is a small residential complex for both single and married-family student housing, and the College struggles annually to fill the 600 beds that they offer. In the late-1980s, the College began offering a limited sports program primarily to help with student recruitment.

The basketball and baseball teams have had a strong success in the National Junior College Athletic Association, but the women's Swimming and Diving team is the most well-known, winning the NJCAA national championship five times between 1997 and 2005. Despite the sprawling city, WCC is the pride of many, particularly among the blue-collar, working class who learned their trades and got their start due to the open-access policy of the College.

Dr. Gladys Evangeline is the president of WCC, having grown up in Pine City, the daughter of a manufacturing company president. Although she went to college out of state, her 20 year tenure at WCC had been marked with numerous accomplishments and few blemishes. A strong political ally to anyone across town in the State House, she once declared her commitment to WCC by saying "If our men's hockey team wins tonight, I'll get a tattoo of them on my shoulder!" The WCC Mountain Goats won that evening, and in a very public display, Dr. Evangeline had the Mountain Goat mascot with a hockey stick tattooed to the back of her shoulder.

WCC, through its charter, is an open-access institution that will accept anyone in the five county region who holds a high school diploma or GED. The College's history in job training programs has played a dominant role for the College, but increasingly, students have enrolled at WCC to complete their two years of general education requirements. For students who have financial concerns, hold jobs, need to attend on a part-time basis, or have struggled academically, WCC has historically been considered a great place to start.

Twelve miles across Pine City is Metropolitan State University, one of the state's two research-oriented universities. With over 150 academic degree programs, a comprehensive medical and dental school, and nearly 35,000 students, MSU is the dominant higher education institution in the state. MSU enrolls students from every county in the state but with a competitive admissions policy, turns down about 30-40% of all applicants each year.

MSU and WCC have enjoyed a mixed relationship on virtually every front for the past 30 years. There was a time in the 1990s when the new WCC Mountain Goat basketball team upset MSU in an exhibition game. There have been taunts about the inferior nature of community college students and their inability to be competitive for admission to MSU, and, MSU has on more than one occasion "poached" the best WCC faculty members. Some of the tensions went as far back as the original founding of WCC, when the MSU president publicly opposed its formation. His argument at the time was that the state could not afford two institutions in the same city and that there would be an inevitable duplication of programs and degrees. He worried that the community college would draw students away from four year schools where statistics showed that students were more likely to get a four year degree if they started at a four year school. The MSU president further argued that any state money should be allocated for the creation of a veterinary school rather than a new community college, especially noting that the state's place in the history of the American west provided a wonderful opportunity to be a leader in equine studies. The state has no veterinary school presently and sends graduates to neighboring states for pursuit of any sort of veterinary career.

As WCC began, and ever since this founding, its leadership has argued that the flagship university was not educating the sons and daughters of the working class in the city and surrounding county, and that as a research-university, it should not be worried about job training, remedial education, and serving as the first point of access for higher education. MSU's admissions policies were too restrictive for many in the area, and WCC founders argued, was more interested in graduate education and seeking external research dollars. WCC was also launched with a very affordable tuition level, almost a quarter of what MSU charged. So despite this difficult and political beginning, WCC has enjoyed great success. MSU has had a steady enrollment since WCC opened, and based on what President Evangeline has reported, the students who enroll at WCC do not even consider MSU; the institutions, she reported in the local paper once, "do not compete for students, but rather, we support each other's work and seek out to serve our citizen groups in different ways."

Let's Pause Here

1. To what extent should public higher education institutions be coordinated and aligned with each other's mission? How might such an alignment be controlled at the state level? And, what impact would this control have on institutional entrepreneurship?
2. How might having two public institutions in the same city duplicate services? How might this same setting impact the competition for scarce resources?
3. Articulate what you would consider the role and mission statements for WCC and MSU. In communicating with the public, how do you differentiate between the two and take a pro/con position for the creation of WCC as *separate* higher education institutions.
4. What, if any, areas of competition can you identify between WCC and MSU? Thinking about comprehensive fund raising programs, highlight where the two institutions might be the most likely to compete for the same donors or dollars.

5. Based on what you know about WCC and MSU, what would you project their primary development emphases to be? Who, as a donor group, would be most likely to respond to these potential donors.

Late last year, President Evangeline attended a dinner at the capitol hosted by the Governor. During the dinner, Evangeline asked casually, "What would you think about us expanding our occupational health programs to include a Bachelor of Science in Nursing. And maybe a couple of social science degrees?" The Governor, mid-meal, responded that he did not see any problem with expanding programs, and indicated that he would continue to strongly support WCCs work in the city. He did mention, though, that WCC "is the workhorse of job training in the city" and that "whatever you do, don't dilute that!"

Evangeline then spoke confidentially to several state senators and representatives, and received strong support for expanding programs, including expanding to offer bachelor's degrees in five or six majors. Despite the confidential nature of these conversations, rumors began to circulate through education committees and among state government personnel that WCC was seriously exploring the possibility of becoming a four-year institution. Workforce leaders, who generally viewed WCC as a great career education partner, began to contact President Evangeline to offer their support, and she was particularly encouraged by those in the fields of Nursing, Accounting, and teaching. The local hospital, desperate for more nurses, informally pledged $500,000 to her for scholarship support for a Bachelor of Science in Nursing program. The informal discussion first came to MSU Chancellor David Hastings as gossip.

"Find out what they're doing over there," Hastings

told his Vice Chancellor for Government Affairs Richard Erie. "Call Evangeline and ask her directly, go over to her office and camp out if you have to, but there is no way on earth that they should be trying to take over our mission!"

Erie did not like delivering the news that he found out. He had called the WCC Vice President, who was a friend of his, and got confirmation that WCC, driven by Evangeline and her locally-elected Board of Trustees, wanted to begin offering bachelor's degrees. They had already planned and got tentative approval (although not official approval) to have Southern State, the only other four-year research university in the state, to offer a Bachelor of Business in Accounting on the WCC campus the coming fall and a BSN the next year.

Hastings decided that he needed to move quickly to put a stop to both plans, the offering of four year degrees at WCC and in particular the immediate offering of a business degree. Hasting's assistant called the meeting, asking Evangeline and her vice presidents to come across town for a two-hour lunch meeting to talk about 'collaboration.' The meeting quickly deteriorated, as Hastings opened his box lunch and the conversation tersely, saying "so I hear you are trying to take over what we do?"

Evangeline might be less polished and academic than Hastings, but she had a long and prominent political heritage in Pine City and around the state. She retorted "we're not trying to take over anything, David, we're just trying to meet the basic needs of everyday citizens who can't afford MSU and who are looking to get jobs and contribute immediately to our City." The two staffs met for three hours as the MSU officials tried to reach an agreement, compromise, or in some way convince WCC to cease its plans. The meeting devolved into a shouting match and nothing was accomplished.

President Hastings returned to his office and wrote an official letter to the Governor, with copies to legislators, department of education personnel, and city officials. He sent an advance copy to the local newspaper and media, outlining what he perceived to be the financial costs as well as the replication of programs that WCC was proposing.

In the letter, Hastings wrote that WCC was behaving as a 'rogue' institution that had only self-interests at heart, that the offering of the same degrees by different institutions was a replication of services that wasted tax-payer money, and that it was a personal agenda by Evangeline to change WCC to a four-year institution. "I believe that the proposal, as discussed, is a personal agenda by President Evangeline in an attempt to create a dynasty for her to oversee as she concludes her career over the next several years. Further, this duplication of programs will most certainly minimize the perceived quality of public higher education in our state."

Evangeline, an avid user of social media, responded to Hastings letter in a blog, noting that "MSU is truly a great, national university with internationally recognized scholars, but their self-interests drive them to meet a global constituent need, and in the process I'm afraid, they have forgotten what it is like to live in Pine City."

No one in government seemed to want to get into the middle of a dispute between the two institutions, and the local newspaper generally sided with WCC, although they reported the dispute between the two institutions as a comical argument between spoiled children. Even the governing boards of the two institutions decided to remain silent and allow the administrations to "fight it out."

With little traction in resolving the dispute, WCC filed its formal paperwork with the state to first allow Southern

State to offer their bachelor's degree on campus for two years, and following that, WCC would change its name to Western College and would expand its programs to offer three bachelor's degree programs. Evangeline's staff also filed paperwork with the regional accrediting body. The plan for expansion included a budget that would minimally increase operating costs, mostly seeing some instructional costs increase and some additional purchasing by the library. WCC would also have to pay a 're-titling fee' of $20,000 with the regional accrediting agency to change its name.

Let's Pause Again

1. Should the possibility of a four year degree delivery program in conjunction with MSU have been explored?
2. Could you have found a compromise position on behalf of MSU that would make both institutions happy?
3. How could MSU trust WCC after surreptitiously and clandestinely going to a competitor, Southern State University, to offer a degree with them? Should WCC's president told her plans to the president of MSU?
4. Does the promise of the local hospital's contribution influence your thinking about WCC's proposal?
5. Develop a philosophy for higher education coordination in your state. How do you propose controlling for institutional 'mission creep' or 'mission denial?'

Hastings felt defeated and frustrated, and opened the Chronicle of Higher Education on his computer to look at what other jobs might be out there for a college president. He noticed Hawaii State's president had resigned, and he looked out at the snow-capped mountains around Pine City and thought of tropical winds and beaches and wondered what could possibly be wrong in Hawaii. He pictured himself as the president there, wearing a Hawaiian shirt to the office, when his daydream was interrupted by a knock on the door.

"Dave, do you have a minute?" asked the Vice President for University Advancement

Jerry Bellows. "I think I've got a possible solution for us," he offered, recognizing that the WCC expansion was the dominant topic of conversation throughout the president's office and pretty much all over campus.

Bellows outlined his strategy. "What if we called together the three most powerful local benefactors in Pine City, all of them are our alumni, as well as donors to both us and WCC." He continued, "if we can show them the WCC plans, what it will cost, what impact it will have on students, and the future of higher education in our state, there is a chance, just a chance, they can balk at it and slow the entire thing down." Hastings was not sure that he liked the idea, but he had run out of options other than updating his curriculum vitae.

Hastings set up the meeting to include his senior team and the three benefactors. He chose a restaurant near the capitol building and reserved the private room for four hours. The benefactors were briefed to the extent that they would have a discussion about college expansions, and even without more information, all of them had seen the mudslinging in the local newspaper. Hastings knew this was a risky meeting, not knowing what the "trio," as they were dubbed, would say or do.

The combined wealth of the three donors was well over $500 million, and all were active not only in higher education with MSU, but throughout the state, funding and influencing all kinds of agendas, ranging from legislative priorities to non-profit charities. Hastings had a small team of staff with him from MSU so as not to intimidate The Trio, but, he was prepared to use any tactic that he might need to prevent WCCs proposed expansion.

"Do they have a leg to stand on?" one of The Trio asked Hastings. "Well, its really a matter of opinion. WCC has done great, great things for job training and providing remedial education, but unless you want Big Government to replicate programs, then it's just not worth it," Hastings explained. "Here's a great example," he continued. "We offer a Bachelor of Science in Nursing on campus, and a program called an RN-to-BSN, so that if you complete an associate's degree and earn your RN, you can complete the BSN through MSU online. It's convenient for the students, it's good for the community, and the students can work full-time and earn the degree while going part-time. It's a win-win for everybody. But Western wants to bring Southern State in to offer a BSN on their campus, just five miles from where we offer our degree program. I think it just sounds like a lot of waste."

The Trio spent the entire four hours reserved in the restaurant talking and breaking down every possible issue they could think of. The Trio, without too much prodding, came to the conclusion that the proposed expansion was indeed duplicating resources and would end up costing them, the tax payers, more money, and that the future was in the efficient offering of programs, not the duplication and competition among programs.

One of the donors asked the MSU staff to leave and indicated that they would come up with a plan and would let Hastings know. Grateful, with the bill paid, the MSU delegation filed out of the back room and as they walked out into the afternoon sunshine, they were shocked to see a photographer and reporter from the local newspaper waiting for them.

"Dr. Hastings, can you tell us what your donors are going to do? Did you call this meeting? Was there an agenda? Did you allow President Evangeline the opportunity to talk to these donors?" The questions came rapid fire from the reporter who followed Hastings to his car. The pictures the newspaper photographer took were uploaded to a Twitter account immediately along with the wording "Hastings calls out big guns in secret meeting." The account was also on the front page of the newspaper the next morning.

The Trio had stayed in the back room of the restaurant for over another hour, and the newspaper reporter and photographer had moved on after catching the MSU delegation leaving. The three donors had supported MSU for nearly 40 years, and $1 million contributions were common among the three, and multiple buildings and rooms were named after them and their business and children around campus. They had a strong, vested interest in MSU being seen as a leading national university, and they decided, strongly, that WCC would not diminish what they had invested in. They each agreed to call the Governor, whom all three knew by his first name, local legislators, and even the Director of the State Department of Education in protest. One of the benefactors, who had under consideration a major proposal from WCC, decided to call President Evangeline and tell her that he would absolutely not fund the proposal should she move forward with her plans.

Hastings did not publicly comment on his meeting with The Trio, but began to see immediate results of their efforts. The Lt. Governor visited campus and in a very public show of support commented on how "The State must continue to make sure MSU is a local, national, and global leader in higher education and that we must do nothing to encumber their growth and success." The Governor and his wife attended a basketball game, wearing MSU school colors, and sat in a special seating area of the arena with two members of The Trio.

The Director of the State Department of Education called WCC President Evangeline early one morning and said, very simply and with a matter of fact tone, "we've been reviewing the WCC proposal for Southern to come on campus, and at the State Board meeting next week, the proposal will be withdrawn. I'm afraid there is strong opposition to the plan, and the Board president would prefer to not even vote on the proposal."

Evangeline had one last opportunity, and called her own largest donor, a large cosmetics manufacturer in the city. The company president, however, declined involvement in the "School House Fight," as the local newspaper called the dispute. WCCs development officer also reported that their gift request to one of the large local foundations, of whom one of "The Trio" sat on the board, had declined to fund their proposal.

Feeling defeated, Evangeline called her colleague at Southern and indicated that she was withdrawing her proposal for program expansion. She then called President Hastings who reluctantly accepted her phone call.

"David, I'm so sorry we couldn't work things out over this degree offering," she started. "But since we have pulled that off the table and are not going to pursue it, we wanted to invite you and your wife over to our hockey game this weekend as our guest." Hastings did not flinch as he accepted the offer, but rolled his eyes as Evangeline finished her invitation with "and maybe we can talk about that gift proposal that we didn't get. You might have some ideas on who else could fund it."

To Conclude the Discussion

1. Should major benefactors be used in this manner for a purely political task? What might be the long term consequences of asking for their involvement in such matters?
2. Is it appropriate to cause a benefactor to refrain from making a contribution to another institution for political expediency? Why or why not, and remember, that it is okay to advocate for an institution or cause that you might believe in.
3. Is WCC really a competitor that a flagship university should worry about? What might the advocacy of program growth at a local community college say about the role and mission fidelity of a near-by four-year institution?
4. What kind of next steps should both institutional leaders be thinking about? Is there something in specific that MSU should begin thinking about changing in terms of their access philosophy? With such a strong show of support from the political establishment, should they begin something new? Should WCC consider developing stronger political alliances with donors? Should they be considering other programmatic changes?
5. From the perspective of a fund raising professional, what lessons might be learned, or developed, to use alumni and donors in assuring institutional welfare? What programs might be used to develop this asset over a long period of time?

Case Study 2:
Paying for the Campaign

Monroe State University is a large public research University located in the eastern United States, only five hours from New York City and five hours from Washington, DC. The institution is a Land Grant University and the leading public institution in the state, and was named after James Monroe, the 5th President of the United States. The student population is approaching 30,000, and has grown rapidly during the past five years. When the state began coordinating higher education institutions in the early-1980's, Monroe State, or MSU for short, retained its independent board of trustees, and with their leadership and support, the university has an annual operating budget of over $2 billion.

MSU relies heavily on their large medical school and hospital complex for funding and research grant support. The medical complex competes on campus for attention with the agricultural college, known throughout the world for agricultural transportation logistics. The agricultural college specializes in dried goods transportation and has produced six Secretaries of Agriculture, more than any other university in America. Additionally, agricultural school faculty are frequently called upon internationally for their work in roadway development and transportation hub creation. But despite the nature of the agricultural disciplines, the university is frequently seen as a "cow college," giving a nod to the historical significance of agriculture at MSU.

In addition to medicine and agriculture, the university has a typical, broad range of academic programs, over 200, in bachelor's through doctoral degree programs, and competes in the NCAA Division I. The university has sporadic success in sports, with perhaps a greater history of success in basketball than any other sport. Additionally, the majority of MSU alumni reside in the Washington-Philadelphia-New York metropolitan area, and although that is geographically compressed, the metropolitan nature of the area makes it difficult for alumni chapters to sustain long-term success.

With a very respectable reputation, the University has not been able to achieve the kind of national respect and attention its leaders desire and believe that it deserves. Many competing and more prestigious institutions call MSU the "Mid-Atlantic Cow College," but most of the performance indicators, from student debt accumulation to graduation rates, suggest that the university is much better than the public realizes. Surrounded by prestigious private eastern colleges and universities, many at MSU have an inferiority complex.

The retirement of a long standing, beloved president gives the institution the catalyst it needs to make a quantum leap in academic rankings and its perception among peers. The independent Board of Trustees hired a new president who was a DC-insider in addition to having a strong academic and fundraising background. The new president, Dr. Henry R. Copeland, recognizes the great importance of a solid, sophisticated fundraising program and has plans to galvanize fundraising and launch a multimillion dollar capital campaign as soon as possible.

President Copeland makes an early, but painful and difficult decision, to replace the Vice President for Advancement with a more seasoned executive he had previously worked with at another institution. The Vice President has been described as a "hard charger" and at times difficult to work with, but is particularly well known for getting results. The university he is coming from has a successful fundraising program and consistently raises over $100 million annually.

The Board of Trustees, as they were exempt from becoming part of the state university system, had been slow to adopt private fund raising practices as a necessity in the 21st century. Additionally, the former President never pressed the need for fundraising with the Board, and the overall assessment by the new Vice President for Advancement was that there was an insufficient culture of fundraising on campus and with the senior institutional leadership. MSU typically raised $40-$50 million per year, about a third of what Copeland believed he needed to transform MSU into the nationally-recognized academic powerhouse he believed possible.

The Board of Trustees quickly got behind Copeland and his new Vice President, and signaled very specifically to the deans and faculty that fundraising must become a priority for the entire campus. Fundraising success, as determined by the Board, would be a criterion for the evaluation of all academic deans, as well as other vice presidents with external stakeholders, such as the Provost, the Vice President for Student Affairs, and even the Vice President for Administration.

The Vice President for Advancement, Jake Carnes, knows he must staff up dramatically for the upcoming campaign as well as find additional resources for general budget augmentation. In fact, preliminary planning seems to suggest that the advancement budget needs an additional $8 million in revenue to be added to a current budget of $12 million. Carnes began to articulate to anyone and everyone, including the Faculty Senate when he was introduced to them, that a "$20 million dollar per year development budget should produce $150 million dollars per year for the university. That means that we are only spending 13-cents on the dollar to help transform MSU."

A professor of psychology openly challenged Carnes at the Faculty Senate meeting, declaring "I don't know where you think you get the right to come onto campus and try and change things like you are. We've been absolutely fine, and with all due respect to you and President Copeland, I think we spend far too much money on these kinds of fancy dinners and parties and travel to begin with!"

Let's Pause Here

1. How do President Copeland or Vice President Carnes respond to the faculty member making the challenge? In what venue should such a response be made, and to what extent do the senior administrators need to begin "selling" the idea of focusing on fundraising at MSU?
2. What kinds of measures might President Copeland consider when evaluating his administrative team, including his deans, on fundraising performance? Is performance in fundraising strictly about the bottom line, how much is raised, or is it more about a continuous process? How would either be measured?
3. Virtually doubling a development budget could be seen from any number of perspectives, including the creation of a bloated administration. How important are inclusive processes of identifying gift funding priorities for the campus? What procedures might be best used for this identification?

4. Vice President Carnes was hired to do a job, and that job is to significantly raise more money for MSU. He has the full support of the President and Board. How concerned should he be about possible opposition from faculty or staff? How concerned should he be about his own job security?
5. If the campus needs an additional $8 million to succeed at fundraising at the level the Board expects, where does President Copeland begin to look for that amount of money?

President Copeland knows that money is not widely available on campus, and wonders if things would have been any different if MSU was part of the larger state system. He doubts it, but does think about the lack of any new monies coming to MSU from the past two Governor's, coming up on eight years. And although budgets have been tight, they have not been entirely restrictive. Enrollment growth has created some additional cash, although most of that added tuition revenue has been directed back to annual operating expense. That means that the President and now the new Vice President have some, but very few additional resources. And although Copeland wants very much to fully fund development he finds that all of the other units also clamor for more money and every dollar allocated toward development is something of a political struggle.

Vice President Carnes wonders at home with his wife about whether or not he made the right decision in coming to MSU. He knew that there would be difficulties, but he thought the entire campus was in agreement that development was a necessity, and he was finding that to be a false assumption almost every day. He found himself meeting with Copeland late in the afternoon, after others had left, to try and strategize some solution to garnering the resources he needs to make fundraising at MSU work. He is also, very confidentially, speaking to some of his friends around the country looking for solutions to his funding problem, as well as asking about other opportunities that might be professionally available.

MSU has an independent 501(c)3 foundation that serves as a banker and investment manager for all funds raised at the University. The organization has a private board of directors and small executive staff. Unlike many university related foundations, the MSU Foundation raises no gift funds and employs no fundraising staff, as all fundraising is handled by the MSU development office in consultation with academic and administrative units. The Foundation does dispense checks and funds to the university and manages the institution's endowment which stands at $515 million. The foundation pays its bills by taking a small allocation of basis points from the endowment. Basis points, Carnes reminded himself, are one hundredth of one percent, or 10% of a penny on the dollar. The MSU administration had negotiated a small allocation of basis points for its fundraising operations a number of years ago, prior to Copeland's arrival and before any of the existing Board members began their service. Both the university and the foundation get 35 basis points from the endowment for operations.

Vice President Carnes decides that he must convince President Copeland, the Board of Trustees, and the Foundation's Board of Directors and Executive Director to increase the basis points he receives for fundraising operations. He has two main tactics in this thinking, the first of which is to benchmark peer institutions and to bring the basis point allocation into alignment with aspirational peers, and the second is that it would be a painless way to raise more money for fundraising operations without hurting anyone or any operation on campus.

Javier Murry, the Executive Director of the Foundation, is very opposed to more basis points for fundraising operations. He has been able to keep his costs low and expects the fundraising arm to do the same thing. Murry specifically notes that instead of following others, they are leading the region in keeping the cost of fundraising dollars low, lowest in fact, among their current peer group.

Copeland called a meeting of Murry and Carnes in his private office. "Gentlemen," Copeland started, "we seem to be at an impasse. I'm quite frankly not sure what to do with Jack's request, and I don't want to force you to do anything you are not comfortable doing financially, Javier."

Javier was quick to respond, "Henry, I have a great respect for what you are doing with MSU, but remember, I report to the Foundation Board, not you. The Board is entirely independent of campus, and I take my orders from them."

Javier also noted that with a spending rate of 5% for academic programs (500 basis points), and another 1% (100 basis points) for investment fund managers and another half-percent (50 basis points) for endowment advisors, there is not much "chicken left on the bone." Inflation also eats away at the endowment at a rate, on average, of 2% a year, Javier Murry noted, which means that the endowment would need to earn a minimum of 9-10% to break even, an unlikely scenario in any economic environment.

Copeland knew Murry was right; the Foundation Board could do whatever it wanted with the allocation amount and it would take a Board vote to change the 35 basis point allocation to campus. He immediately thought of consulting his university legal counsel, but could predict what they would say and it would take him ten times as long to get the answer he knew he would get. The meeting of the three administrators did nothing to change the impasse.

Copeland had a second problem that was starting to arise, and that was the president of the Faculty Senate. Claire Minor, a professor of psychology, was in her second year as president of the Senate, and requested a meeting with Copeland following the last Senate meeting when one of her departmental colleagues challenged Vice President Carnes.

"President Copeland," Minor started, "we are all fans of what you are doing on campus, but there is a growing concern about Mr. Carnes and what he wants to do with development. As you are well aware, faculty salaries are below our aspirational averages, we have facility upgrade issues, faculty travel allocations have been stagnant and hardly cover the cost of a single conference for a full professor. We just can't afford to invest the kind of money Mr. Carnes wants to take from campus."

Let's Pause Again

1. How should President Copeland respond to Claire Minor as President of the Faculty Senate? Should he directly address her concerns, should he put something in writing to respond to the entire faculty? Should he meet with the Faculty Senate leaders and discuss their concerns?
2. What tactic should President Copeland take in working with Javier Murry and the Foundation? Is all hope lost for changing the basis point allocation, or is it worth Copeland's time to meet with Foundation

Board members to explain his position and hope for a different outcome?

3. How would you advise Jack Carnes as he runs into this roadblock? He was hired to specifically raise more money and understands what he needs to accomplish this, and is now being told that he cannot have the resources he needs. What reaction should he have as a professional and as a friend and colleague to President Copeland?

4. Copeland's efforts to increase fundraising is ultimately about bringing more financial resources to campus. Who would be his key constituents in trying to convey this message? Draft an email to these constituents explaining in a convincing fashion what Copeland's goals are.

5. What options do you think that Copeland and Carnes have? Map out these strategies and list specific action steps for each one, and then identify what you believe to be the most realistic possible direction for them to take.

President Copeland was frustrated after his meeting with Minor and hearing her concerns from the Faculty Senate. "Why don't they understand what we are trying to do will solve their problems," he wondered to himself and to anyone within earshot. He knew that if they doubled or tripled their annual fundraising, issues like travel and capital construction and renovation could be helped considerably. Even creating endowed professorships would help with travel and would elevate salaries. Why didn't the Faculty Senate see that? He invited Carnes to his home for a glass of wine after work to talk and think through what they might be able to do.

"Jack, I'm frustrated. I'm not sure what our next step

should be," Copeland said to his friend as he poured the wine. "We have to find a way to make this work. This is institutional culture change 101, right?"

"Henry, if we can't put something together in the next couple of months," Jack responded, "I'm going to head back over to DC. "I'd rather be here with you, I really love this place, but if we can't begin to staff our development program, then there is no way we can put together the fundraising program that MSU has the potential to have."

Carnes opened his briefcase and pulled out a notepad. "Henry, what do you think our options really, truly are to come up with at least $5 million?" The two leaders came up with the following list of options:

1. Create a line-item budget for the entire University.

The University currently works from an incremental budgeting perspective where each unit gets an increase or decrease of some set percentage. An option that President Copeland could use would be to have each funded unit breakdown their budget into specific categories and justify these. This is a version of zero-based budgeting, where essentially 'packages' are developed with expenses requested. By creating this type of budgeting, the President could cut or take money away from individual programs that do not meet some viability threshold. Copeland recognizes that this would be extremely difficult, as it would essentially be seen as a 'shell-game,' where money is just re-distributed and there could be the possibility of perceptions of favoritism. However, the Board has agreed with the President that fundraising is a major priority, thus giving the Copeland a mandate of sorts to make the operation successful.

2. Consolidation of unrestricted gifts

A common practice in many universities is the consolidation of unrestricted gifts to the campus being centralized and controlled by one office or source. MSU receives about $2-4 million in unrestricted gifts each year, and they currently are assigned to the accounts that are managed and controlled by academic colleges. For example, an accounting graduate might give $100 to an unrestricted account. The current practice is that the money is directed to a business college unrestricted account, and changing that would mean that the gift would go to the university's unrestricted account that could then be immediately redirected to the development office to pay for whatever operating costs they might incur. The academic colleges that receive the unrestricted money use it for all kinds of things, including aiding faculty travel, paying for retreats, consultants, and planning, and even holiday parties and receptions. They also rely on it significantly for their own alumni and development work, and changing the practice of allocating the money away from academic units would be met with resistance. On top of that, there could be legal issues in re-designating dollars restricted to academic units.

3. Implementation of a gift tax

A common practice for many higher education institutions is to charge a fee to each gift that is made to the institution to finance the administration of fundraising activities. Although many benefactors do not typically look upon gift "taxes" favorably, they have been considered legal and appropriate if handled correctly. A portion of an individual's gift is used for operational support, and although large donors may balk at the percentage of a gift that goes to administrative services, most smaller donors have no idea that a 'gift tax' even exists. This practice is common throughout the non-profit world, and colleges and universities are far from unusual in implementing these kinds of fees. Most non-profits also publicly report the percentage of cost that is used to raise each dollar. MSU currently uses a small portion of donor gifts to help finance the fundraising operation, but proudly boasts that 97% of each dollar raised goes directly to the purpose of the gift. The benchmark that Carnes seems to remember is that most higher education institutions report something closer to 90%.

4. Gift float

Copeland and Carnes also recalled the notion of "gift floating." Some universities deliberately hold funds that might otherwise be designated to particular units of the organization for expenditure for as long as 90 days. Some institutions hold the funds for an even longer period, 6 months to a year. During the holding period the organization invests the funds and uses the interest to help finance development operations. This "float" can provide substantial resources to help defray fund raising costs.

5. Unrestricted bequests

A bequests is a gift that is legally transferred to an institution from an estate, will, or trust. Copeland can count three wills that were executed during the past year where the donors simply indicated that they wanted to leave something like "half of their estate to MSU." Often, these are alumni who have not been in contact with the university in many years, but remember it fondly. There are also a number of sports-fanatics who do not specify in their estates that they want the funds to go directly to athletics. The practice at MSU has been to try and sort out and make best guesses as to where the money should be directed, but Copeland and Carnes have the thought that they could direct these bequests to an unrestricted account to pay for development expansion. They also had the thought that they could take only a percentage of the bequests and assign the remainder to the accounts using the best-guess method that they had been using.

As President Copeland and Vice President Carnes finished their bottle of wine, they believed that they had a realistic set of options to get the necessary money to fund the development operation. Copeland knew that he would first have to visit with the Board chair, then his executive team, and then the rest of the board before he unveiled any plans. Any of the plans could cause a major stir among the faculty, deans, and staff, he wanted to be certain that he had full administrative and leader support before he made any change.

To Conclude the Discussion

1. Based on the five alternatives Copeland and Carnes identified, how would you advise them to proceed? What are the benefits, risks, and disadvantages of each of the five strategies? How might each of these impact donor behavior or perception of the university?
2. Should Copeland just make an executive decision to reallocate money through the traditional budgeting process? Would such an action be seen as 'strong leadership' or 'dictatorial behavior?' What would either approach indicate to his executive team?
3. What role should the Foundation play in making this decision? Should Javier Murry be consulted before Copeland has any discussion with the Board chair? Should the Foundation remain silent and simply fol-

low the directions of Copeland and the University, or should they protest for their individual beliefs?

4. Virtually any of the possible solutions Copeland has will make some constituent potentially unhappy. How would you advise him to develop support for his plan throughout the university community? What about for the donor community?

5. What are the consequences for Copeland if he does not have consensus and buy-in from the campus community regarding how to fund the capital campaign and development structure?

6. Is it possible you might decide to use all of the modes of financing the campaign?

Case Study 3:
Two Donors, One Building

Southern College of Art and Design is a well-established private college with a curriculum built around the arts, design, and the creative arts. Although the College has a strong liberal arts program, mostly emphasizing the humanities, the College is known nationally for its emphasis on early declaration of majors by their freshmen and their strong business and industry ties. The film program, in particular, often sees students interning with Hollywood studios filming movies in the southeast. The student body is small, only 1,400 students, and, as a private institution, is tuition dependent and there is a strong reliance on external fund raising programs to keep programs relevant and on the cutting-edge.

Although Southern is located in the deep-south, students enroll from all over the nation because of its superb reputation. While expensive, the School boasts very competitive admissions standards and only accepts students who have strong academic backgrounds and show great talent and promise. Southern is also unique because it uses a portfolio admissions process for admission to many of the fine and performing arts degree programs, and one faculty member recently commented that "Southern has the pick of only the very best students from around the country."

A small number of students do actually become paint and sculpture artists, but the vast majority of students enter the world of work for corporate entities who are looking for product or graphic designers. The job market is good for Southern graduates with some students actually being offered two or three jobs from different companies. Corporations recruit heavily on campus, and there are many offices, lounges, and classrooms around campus named for these corporations who have also made large contributions to the college.

In the mid-1970s the Emerson Family donated numerous works of "primitive art" to the college that reportedly were worth several million dollars at the time. The primitive art movement in the south was particularly popular in the mid- and late-1800's, and was heavily influenced by the slave population as well as plantation owners. The collection included 25 paintings, some of them quite large, and several of the artists had gone on to some fame.

The Emerson family is a prominent local family that made their fortune in tobacco farming. With a lineage that dates back to the 1700s, they are among the oldest continuous families in the south, and although several members of the family had gone to college at Southern, many had also gone to college in the northeast. The family's connection to Southern was one of proximity; Southern was simply "the college in the neighborhood."

When the family patriarch, Robert D. Emerson, made the gift of art, he did not include any funds for the upkeep or storage of the art, but he had thought about how it would, could, or should be displayed. At the time, he did not offer to include cash in his gift to Southern to build a facility to display the art, but strongly hoped that one day the college would build something with the Emerson family name on it. All who worked at the college at the time understood that that Mr. Emerson had wanted to have an "Emerson Family Art Museum" on the Southern campus. Several years after making the art donation, Mr. Emerson wrote to the college president indicating that he hoped to one day fund a "world class art museum" that would "allow Southern to display this fine collection of art and recognize the individuals who expressed themselves so vividly." With the decline in tobacco sales, especially by the late-1980s, the Emerson family fortune was not what it once was. The result was Mr. Emerson's comment in the letter "I do so very wish that I could now write you a check to build this art museum, but unfortunately, our current state of assets prevents us from making such a donation. I do ask, however, that before anyone else be allowed to build and name an art museum for this collection that you consult with me or my family first and provide us the opportunity to provide a gift to name the building."

When Mr. Emerson made the gift of artwork, the college had honored him and his family with a luncheon and highlighted the placement of the artwork around campus with a brochure and walking tour that was called "The Emerson Art Tour." By the mid-1980s, the brochures had become dated, and by the mid-1990s, even locating a brochure became a problem. The Emerson Collection was still noted as a point of pride for the college, but had become something of an after-thought to most working at the college, including the constantly changing college administrators. Being a college of art and design, though, the college did place great value on all of its art collections, and from a time when no one can actually pinpoint, there has been an emphasis on trying to build an art museum on campus. An additional benefit of the collection is its sheer value, now in the tens of millions of dollars, as an institutional asset that helps assure the loan capacity of the institution.

Let's Pause Here

1. What do you perceive to be the institution's responsibility to the social implications of highlighting art work created by slaves and given by former slaveholders? Are the ethical considerations that the college administrators and leaders should consider, and if so, how should these be communicated to the campus and larger community?

2. What do you think an effective long-term recognition strategy should be for significant donors? Does an institution have a responsibility to continue its stewardship of a donor for multiple generations, and does your response here change based on whether or not the gift was from a family versus an individual?

3. Discuss the value of contributions of property such as the art collection that was given. Develop a listing of pro's and con's of receiving gifts of property. What long-term considerations should be discussed prior to accepting such a gift?

4. What impact does the naming of classrooms and lecture halls have on the creation of a 'culture of giving' at an institution? How can such a culture be developed and articulated to students, as well as alumni and staff? What do you see as the real value of a naming opportunity?

5. The Emerson collection is something that the College values, at very least for its cash value and what that brings to the overall assets of the institution. What responsibility does a new college president have for learning about gifts like this, and at what threshold or

what criteria would you advocate for president's to use in making a determination about learning about these historic gifts?

Jock Stucker had worked his way up in the development office to the position of Vice President for Development. He began as the Director of Annual Giving, moved into Major Gifts, and found himself in Planned Giving before being promoted into the Vice Presidency six years ago. When Dr. Jennifer L. Cotton was hired two years ago as the college's President, she kept him in the role for strategic reasons. Cotton had been hired from a similar school in Miami, and she wanted someone with a good institutional history and memory on her team.

Almost as part of his upbringing, he believed that an art museum or gallery should be a major component in their capital campaign. The feasibility studies he participated in bore that idea, as the vibrant art community naturally saw Southern playing a major role in the arts. As campaign materials were developed, and as President Cotton began her work, a new building housing a Museum of Art was included as a high priority. Additionally, some of the language included a centralized location for housing the Emerson art collection.

Stucker has remained close to several members of the Emerson family, but their interactions were largely ceremonial or casual. The family continued to make smaller gifts, and one member of the family continued to give $5,000 a year. There is little evidence that the family has the potential to fund the $10 million proposed art museum, and there seems to be little interest in participating in any major way with the college. Robert Emerson's three children are included in many invitation lists, but on average, one child might attend one event a year, and with little regularity.

When Cotton arrived at Southern, she was briefed by Stucker on a long list of major donors for her to meet and formally introduce herself. No Emerson relative was on that list. In one meeting with her development staff, Cotton asked Stucker "Tell me about the Emerson family and this art collection?" Stucker had to admit that he knew of the family and their place in local history, but that "they aren't active donors or prospects right now. Their family gave the art, and we try to include them, but there's not much there we can do anything with."

Cotton recognized the growing value of the artwork, but also the uncomfortable history of slave-owning and the broad, national discussions of primitive art and its rightful ownership. Although no legal battles had reverted ownership of slave produced art, she was aware that it was probably a good idea to keep the collection together, well curated, and under control. In her two years as President, though, there has been no formal reference to the Emerson collection other than what she has noted and instigated, that is until she received a completely unexpected phone call.

"Dr. Cotton," the voice began, "I do apologize for not coming to introduce myself, but my name is Clement Morton, and my wife, Abby and I, are very interested in supporting Southern with a possible gift for your art collection." They spoke informally for a few minutes and made an appointment for lunch the following day.

Cotton was briefed on the Morton family, and neither Clement nor his wife had much of a giving history to Southern. At lunch, they talked easily and Dr. Cotton felt she was at the apex of her 'game' in relating to the Morton's. Both Cotton and the Mortons found out over lunch that they knew some of the same people in Florida, and Clement felt confident and relaxed when he took his wife Abby's hand and said, "Jennifer, we have thoroughly enjoyed having lunch with you today, but we seem to have avoided what we came here to talk about. Abby and I grew up in this city and are very much committed to the arts, and want to help out Southern by making a significant gift to the college for your art collection. Specifically, I would like to see a building for the art collection, and with your permission, name it after my wife, Abby." Abby blushed slightly but then kissed her husband's hand.

Cotton expected as much and was thrilled with the news and what appeared to be such a wonderful, loving elderly couple. She responded with gratitude, "oh, thank you so much. The college is very grateful for this kind of support. But you do know that our projections for an art museum are around $8-$10 million."

Clement Morton didn't bat an eye when he responded, "yes, I know. I have some stock for the gift, but the majority of it would be a cash gift." Jennifer graciously accepted the verbal commitment of the gift, indicating that renderings of the building could be made available soon for them to see, and the three left the restaurant with warm feelings of accomplishment.

As Cotton drove back to her office, she excitedly called Vice President Stucker, "we've got the art museum! The Abby Morton Museum of Art!" The two agreed to meet in person to go over a draft of what the gift agreement would look like later that afternoon, and Stucker went to work with his research department to do a deep-level of research on Mr. and Mrs. Clement Morton. What he found was troubling.

That afternoon, Stucker walked directly into Cotton's office and did not hesitate to lead with his problem. "I think we might have a glitch," he said. "Turns out that Abby Morton is actually 'Abagail Finis Davis Morton,' the great, great granddaughter of Jefferson Finis Davis, the President of the Confederacy during the Civil War. President Cotton groaned loudly. "Hey, but at least you haven't accepted the gift yet" Stucker added.

"Well, about that," Cotton started. "I told them thank you and that I do accept it. And what do you think? Do you think we shouldn't take it based on something that happened 150 years ago?"

Stucker responded quickly that if she verbally accepted the gift, then they probably should proceed with accepting it. Stucker had an idea to create a couple of focus groups, and assembled three groups of students and three groups of community members to talk about their impressions of the funding. He spent the entire day talking to the focus groups and even had his Associate Vice President running an online poll, all hopefully without the knowledge of the Morton's. By the end of the day, Stucker was pleased to report that no one seemed too overly concerned with the source of the gift, and he further recommended that they use the name "Abby Morton Museum of Art."

Under Cotton's authority, Stucker and legal counsel drew up the gift agreement and after several phone calls to the Morton's, arranged for a public announcement and signing of the agreement the following week.

Let's Pause Again

1. Was President Cotton correct to verbally accept the Morton gift? If not, what course of action should she have taken and would there have been a risk of losing the gift or seeming ungrateful to the Morton's if she hesitated?

2. How would you approach the 'Abby Morton' history? Would you publicly disclose her family's history? What wording could you use to frame her family's history so that it encourages discourse, but does not illicit negative, Civil War and slavery emotions?
3. How much research is enough for a donor meeting? Should Stucker have identified the family history of Abby prior to the lunch meeting? How can a senior level executive, such as the President, best prepare for these kinds of meetings with individuals who claim they are interested in making significant contributions?
4. Should President Cotton be up-front with the Morton's about the background work they did before accepting the gift? Does she run the risk of losing the gift if they find out that the college ran focus groups about the appropriateness of Abby's family history?
5. If you were advising a professional group of fund-raising professionals, what kind of ethical standards would you advocate for in relation to both working with donors and the social responsibilities of colleges and universities?

As Stucker prepares for the press conference, he re-opens a digitized fund raising folder on his desktop about the 'art museum,' not really remembering what all was in it. He finds pdf files of numerous lists of potential donors and matching donors, and then opens a pdf file labeled "Emerson letter." He is shocked and horrified to find that he had completely forgotten about the old 'letter of first refusal.' Jock recognizes the problem immediately and calls President Cotton on her cell phone.

"Jennifer, I have to ask you this first, and will explain second," he said with his heart pounding. "Is there any chance that you called any of the Emerson family before you accepted the Morton gift?"

Confused and a bit anxious, her response of 'no' did nothing to calm the situation. Stucker said "I need 15 minutes of your time right now." He bounded up the stairs to the president's office and walked in to President Cotton sitting at her desk signing letters, still holding her cell phone from their seconds-earlier phone call.

"So here is the deal," Jock said as he walked into the room, sitting at her conference table instead of her desk. "A long time ago, the Emerson family gave that art work, you know that. But, the old man who made the gift, also wanted to name an art museum to house it."

"Sounds familiar," President Cotton said as she sat down at the conference table. "But what does that have to do with the here and now, and tomorrow's press conference?"

"Turns out," Stucker said, "that the family wrote this letter of first refusal, meaning that they have the right to make a gift to house the art collection first, and that we have to let them know before we accept any other gift."

Perturbed, Cotton responded, "So what are the details? I don't remember any big gifts coming from the Emerson family and only vaguely recall their giving. They don't come to many events, do they? I kind of remember a face, but I'm not certain."

Stucker produced a giving history and the contents of his paper file on the Emerson family. From his notes, he could identify Danny Emerson (Robert D. Emerson, III) as the primary contact for the family. He was Robert Emerson's grandson. "I think you've got to call him, like right now," Stucker said.

Cotton thought for a minute about her situation, and agreed that she needed to make the phone call as soon as possible. She mapped out a short conversation with Danny Emerson, and figured she would then need to call the Morton's and just give them a heads-up on the Emerson family situation, and, on top of that, she had several appointments booked back-to-back for the rest of the day. She hoped that she could get Danny Emerson on the first phone call, and she looked at her watch. Just before 3 in the afternoon; she wondered if she could have it all finished by 8 that evening.

Jennifer told Stucker that she would keep him informed and asked him to find any other background information on the Emersons that might be helpful. As Stucker left, she indicated that she was running 15 or 20 minutes behind to her assistant, and closed the door. She sat at her desk, looking out over the Spanish-moss covered trees of the college. A deep breath, and she dialed Danny Emerson's phone number from her desktop telephone.

The phone answered on the third ring. "Hello, Mr. Emerson, this is Jennifer Cotton, I'm president of Southern College of Art and Design. How are you this afternoon," she paused for recognition.

"Yes, I think we've met before," Danny responded somewhat curious about the phone call, certainly apprehensive.

"Yes, I think we have. I have to admit it's been a while, though. I've been here for just two years, and to be honest, I've met so many wonderful people I sometimes have a hard time keeping everyone straight." She hoped the attempt at humor would lighten the mood of the phone call.

"Jennifer, I'm sorry, but I'm in the middle of a discussion right now, can we talk a bit later in the afternoon." Cotton wanted to get this over with, but wanted his full attention to close the conversation once and for all.

"Certainly, is there a time that is good for you?" she

responded. Danny Emerson wanted to put the phone call off until the end of the week, but she pressed the issue. They would talk at 6 PM, much later than she wanted and not leaving much time for her to get in touch with the Morton's or make any plans for the next day. Such phone scheduling was common, she had found. And they made plans to speak later that day.

When Cotton was finally able to speak with Emerson that evening, he was less than friendly to open their conversation. Recognizing that there was not a particularly easy way to introduce the topic, she dove into the story, not using the Morton name, expecting the situation to be resolved with perhaps unhappy, but not unpleasant, feelings.

Emerson exploded with anger, yelling at Cotton that the college was trying to "once again" belittle his family's support for the institution and that the "complete lack of respect for the Emerson family name" was both "humiliating and demeaning." He further contended that the sizeable gift of art should be housed in the Emerson art museum, that he and his family have never been adequately thanked for their gift, and that this recent "slap in the face" is just another indication of their poor treatment by the college. Emerson threatens a lawsuit to take back the artwork.

Cotton tries unsuccessfully to reconcile the situation, but nothing that she said could be heard by an increasingly angry and vocal Danny Emerson. The phone call ends at 6:45 with the threat of a lawsuit.

To Conclude the Discussion

1. What should President Cotton's first action be? How would you advise her to proceed? How soon should

Cotton call the Morton's, and do you believe that this threatens the Morton gift? Should the museum be named for the Morton family or the Emerson family?

2. Given the multi-million dollar gift of art from the Emersons, should the college have been more appreciative through the years and given them some naming opportunity elsewhere on campus?

3. Did Mr. Emerson's letter 25 years ago have any real standing with the University? Were the contents of the letter null and void after the original Mr. Emerson died? Should they have been? Has the fact that 25 years have passed changed any obligation the college has for naming the building after the Emersons?

4. Should the Emerson family be given the opportunity to come forward with a $10 million pledge or gift? If so, how do Stucker or Cotton explain that to the Morton's without jeopardizing their gift?

5. Is Stucker at fault in not identifying the letter earlier? Should he be disciplined for not remembering the letter? Is there any action that Cotton should take regarding Stucker? Should Vice President Jock Stucker have been more insistent that a call be made earlier? What can be done to prevent such problems from arising in the future?

Case Study 4:
Angry Heirs

On the flat plains of the mid-west, Greystone State University is a comprehensive university, founded originally as a state teachers "normal" school. In the late-1960s, as graduate programs began to emerge, the Governor, a graduate of GSU, along with a strong push from alumni, changed the name of the institution from Greystone State Normal College to Greystone State University. As with many institutions of this genre, GSU had a combination of traditional, gothic architecture along with many modern buildings. The university grew dramatically in the 1960's and 1970's from 6,000 to 10,000 students, and over the past decade, has again experienced an enrollment growth to just over 15,000 students.

With a steady enrollment growth, the university offers a typical, broad range of comprehensive university programs, stressing the social sciences. The business school has grown considerably, and is known for accounting, and the rural nursing program is noted as one of the best in the region. The university has several outreach centers around their corner of the state, and the college works hard to articulate degree programs with the state's community colleges. Additionally, the college has a joint degree program with the state land grant university in engineering. GSU has a department of engineering that includes programs in civil and mechanical engineering, but the degree is formally granted from the land grant university 250 miles away.

The message GSU focuses on is providing access and a residential experience for students in the region. The average ACT score varies, but typically is around 23, and there is a strong representation of first generation college students. As with many areas on the Great Plains, there are small minority enrollments,but the growing Hispanic agricultural workforce has prompted a considerable rise in minority student enrollment. The college relies heavily on state and federal financial aid programs, as over 85% of the enrollment receives some type of public financial aid.

The host town of the college is a typical small college town of 30,000. With a strong German and northern European immigrant tradition, the town supports an unusually high number of bakeries and brew-pubs, many marketing on the area's history. Several restaurants and bakeries, however, date back nearly 100 years, and tourists pull off of the interstate to pick up their products or eat a meal there. As the university is the largest employer for over 200 miles in any direction, the community is supportive and relies on GSU as their main economic engine. As a small town, though, there is little in the way of financial support that it can provide to the university.

And, as with many mid-western states, the economic growth has been conservative and the legislature has held constant state funding. Holding constant has been seen as a good thing, but that has also meant that little new money has been infused into the institution, and salaries have been stagnant and capital renovations on now 50 year old buildings is becoming a significant institutional liability.

The development and advancement functions of GSU only date back to the 1980's, and despite efforts to modernize a very manual system, they raise $4 to $6 million annually. The development staff is largely 'home-grown,' meaning that they either went to college at GSU or grew up in the town and have remained to work for the campus. Many staff members wear 'multiple hats,' meaning that they have multiple job assignments that would typically be separated at larger institutions. For example, the Director of Annual Giving is also the Director of Major Gifts, and the planned giving officer also handles corporate and foundation giving. Although innovative and willing to try new things, the entire fundraising program is not overly complex, and they work with local attorneys on estates that are complex or complicated.

A cornerstone of the community for nearly 100 years is the Reinhold Company, one of a very few light manufacturing companies in the region. The company is wholly owned by the Reinhold family, and was founded by Beatrice and Eric Reinhold. Both sets of their parents immigrated to the US from Germany in the 1920's, and were initially attracted to the Great Plains for farming. Beatrice Reinhold was seen as something of a very modern woman, as she helped found the company with her husband, working to develop the processes and workflow in the early years of the company, and took sole control of the corporation two years ago when her husband Eric passed away from cancer. She is 82 years old and in reasonable health, still living in their 'prairie box' home down the street from the factory offices. She still walks to work every day, and begins her day with a German coffee, cheese, and a local 'wurst' or sausage that is sold at a local deli.

The Reinhold Company makes conveyors for agriculture uses, primarily grains, corn, and wheat. Although the rise in corporate farming has changed the need for their products, they continue to be one of the leading companies of its type in the mid-west. The modest lifestyle of the Reinhold family, along with the long term success of the company has made the Reinhold family quite wealthy, particularly Beatrice Reinhold who is a millionaire many times over. Despite her wealth, her demeanor, style, and self-presentation do not reflect her or her family's wealth.

Beatrice has four children and six grandchildren. All of her children work for the company in various capacities, with two in executive positions and two still managing sections of the manufacturing process. They are all well paid and share in substantial bonuses at year end. She has also set up trusts for each grandchild for the eventual payment of tuition to any college or university of their choice.

About five years ago, Mrs. Reinhold began discussions with the president of GSU about her desire to possibly make a significant gift to the institution for the founding of an engineering school, perhaps naming it after her late husband. Neither Beatrice nor Eric had gone to college, and both had regretted not having a formal education; food on the table had been more important. She believed strongly in higher education and modestly supported all three institutions where her children attended. None of her children had gone to GSU, but she and her late husband had a deep affection for the school. Before her husband passed away, they had been approached by the other universities where their children had attended to make some 'significant' gift to those schools, and had even been visited by the school presidents, but they never gave particularly large gifts to any of these institutions. The family had been very generous to their small synagogue and other local philanthropies, illustrating a high level of generosity to causes that they believed in.

Let's Pause Here

1. Develop a strategy for possibly asking Mrs. Reinhold for a significant gift? What steps or actions would you identify to cultivate her interest in GSU? What kinds of messaging would you focus your attention on, and who on your staff would you assign to work most closely with her?
2. What do you consider to be the benefits and disadvantages of a small development staff? What kinds of morale issues might you predict could arise in such a setting, and how would you, as the lead development officer, work to assure a professionally competent and enthusiastic staff?
3. GSU's setting is not unusual; small, rural town, fighting for attention from the land grant university, etc. What kinds of strategies can you identify that might give GSU a competitive advantage in certain areas? How can these advantages be used for development purposes?
4. Do you think of the Reinhold's as a potential family donor or a potential business donor? Does this perception make any difference in how you would cultivate Mrs. Reinhold or the outcome from such a cultivation?
5. Mrs. Reinhold has suggested making a gift for an engineering school, and GSU has a department of engineering. As a development officer, how do you begin to think about this as a realistic or unrealistic possibility? Whom do you consult with after learning about her interest?

The President of GSU is Dr. Steve Larson, a person who grew up not far from GSU. He went away to school, but came back to his 'hometown' five years ago to serve as the President of the university. He never knew Mr. Reinhold very well, but played sports for the next town along the interstate, and knew of the Reinhold kids. Getting acquainted with Mrs. Reinhold was not difficult, but he was a bit surprised when Mrs. Reinhold suggested the engineering school. He explained that founding an engineering school, growing it from a department, would be very expensive.

"How much?" asked Beatrice.

"Well, I would have to really look at salaries, and it would depend on whether we stayed with civil and mechanical engineering, and without looking at it too closely, I would estimate about $50 million to do it right."

Larson knew Mrs. Reinhold was wealthy, but did not think that she was comfortable enough to fund a $50 million gift. Additionally, he had other ideas for her giving, and was looking at her to balk at the number to suggest something else, particularly a need-based scholarship fund for first generation college students in the area.

Larson and Mrs. Reinhold met for coffee occasionally to discuss her possible gift, and whenever Larson began to nudge in the direction of scholarships or any specific action, Mrs. Reinhold seemed to hold back. Frustrated, he asked the Vice President for Development to take up the cultivation. Larson was not convinced that Reinhold was serious about a gift, but did not want to lose out, just in case. Assigning Vice President Jonathon Scarsdale to Mrs. Reinhold was a good strategy, the thought, as the Scarsdale family had been prominent in the community for nearly the same length of time as the Reinholds. And, Scarsdale was the same age and had gone to school with some of Mrs. Reinhold's grandchildren.

For two years, Jonathon met with Beatrice, and the two talked about everything possibly imaginable, including her desire to retire and step away from the company. Although she was still the sole owner, she rarely handled the operational, daily matters of running the business. Beatrice was planning a 21-day trip with several other women from her synagogue to Alaska, and had her assistant call Jonathon for a meeting before she left.

Beatrice was more open than normal, and confessed that she was not in particularly good health and that she needed to have a 'procedure' when she returned from Alaska. She asked Jonathon to keep news of her health private. She again brought up the desire to make a major gift to GSU, a topic that came up from time to time, but rarely with any sort of direct action associated with their conversation.

"Jonathon," Beatrice began, "you have been so good to me for the past couple of years. I want you to know that I really do want to give something big to Greystone. Such a wonderful school. Eric really wanted Greystone to have a school of engineering, and I want to see that happen. With his name on it. How much do you think it would cost. Really?"

"Well, we haven't talked about this too specifically, but I know that President Larson at one point estimated about $50 million. That's a lot of money."

"Could I pay for half of it now and part from my estate, after I'm gone, with a real provision that it be the Eric Reinhold College of Engineering?" Beatrice asked.

Jonathon was astounded and replied "of course." Beatrice was worried about her health, and asked "Can I just write you a note or letter, on letterhead, telling you I want to do this?" She then added that she was doing some estate planning 'cleaning up,' and that her attorney would be sure to put the language in her trust for the gift.

Not quite knowing what to do, Jonathon agreed to

everything, both excited and a little bit uneasy. He had done some work in this area, and thought that he 'knew enough to be dangerous.' He had worked with a donor a couple of years ago and knew that Beatrice could make a "contract to make a will," or as some call it, an "estate note" and that they would work on the trust language as soon as she returned from Alaska. This was agreed to, and Beatrice had her personal assistant come into her office and notarize the document.

Let's Pause Again

1. Is Jonathon correct to accept the gift? What are the academic ramifications of accepting a gift of this nature, and to what extent should others on campus be involved in making the decision to accept or not accept the gift?

2. Is accepting the gift at this moment the best course of action? With Beatrice leaving on vacation so soon, would it be wiser to wait until she returns to resume the discussion?

3. Beatrice, as the donor, is very clear about what she wants to fund. To what extent does it make a difference about this being a priority for the campus? How does this impact GSU's role in the state landscape of higher education?

4. Create a list of talking points that you can share with President Larson about the gift, how it will be funded, and the impact on campus. What questions might the media ask in relation to the announcement of this gift?

5. What does the intention of making the gift do to the "friendship" of Jonathon and Beatrice? Even after she makes the gift, does he continue to meet with her on a regular basis now that she has indicated her desire to

make a gift? What stewardship strategies might you begin to map out as she completes her gift?

The fourth day of the Alaskan trip, near Nome, Alaska, Mrs. Reinhold suffers a massive heart attack and is airlifted to an ICU ward in Anchorage. Her health stabilizes, and she is able to take and make phone calls, and reports feeling much better. She spends a considerable amount of time on the telephone with her children and feeling recovered, decided to call Jonathon. She tells Jonathon by phone that she absolutely intends to fund the school of engineering and to accelerate the creation of appropriate documents to make it happen.

After 6 days in the hospital, Mrs. Reinhold is released and is flown to Seattle to begin preparations for her transportation home. Despite excellent health care facilities, she suffers a second heart attack while in Grey-Sloan Hospital and dies. Mrs. Reinhold's lawyer had not had time to complete her trust document, and she died "intestate." The only evidence of Mrs. Reinhold's intentions were verbal conversations with her lawyer, Jonathon and Dr. Larson, as well as the estate note that her assistant had notarized.

The Reinhold children recognize that their family firm has struggled over the past several decades, but that it had largely survived because of the thrifty nature of both Mr. and Mrs. Reinhold. They had concerns about the long term viability of the company, but also knew that their entire livelihood depended on the manufacturing firm continuing to be profitable. They did not have a good grasp of their mother's financial wealth until a post-funeral discussion with their mother's attorney revealed her considerable wealth.

The Reinhold children listened intently as the attorney spelled out a proposed distribution plans for Beatrice's wealth, including what they would have to pay in inheritance tax. He then presented the notarized estate note and presented a second scenario for the distribution of Beatrice's wealth.

The children listened stoically as the attorney presented his interpretation of options to them, and they asked for him to leave the conference room in which they sat. Upon his departure, they were furious, using language like "those GSU gold-diggers" and "no way on earth" that they would let GSU have nearly all of their mother's estate. Once they calmed down, they also discussed the implications for the future of the company, and that with a direction of some of the capital back into the company, they could modernize significantly and improve profits. They could do that and have some personal savings cushion added to their lives, along with maybe a trip or two, or property or two, in Hawaii. The all agreed completely that there was no way that they would recognize the estate note.

Jonathon felt caught between a rock-and-a-hard-place. He knew the powerful transformation of the gift, he knew of his word to Beatrice, and he was very certain of her intentions. He respected the family, though, and felt that maybe, just maybe, they also had a case, but that they should have had more open discussions with their mother if they wanted to count on her assets to bankroll their vacations.

President Larson was furious that Jonathon had let a gift of that magnitude slip through his hands and blamed him for his sloppy handling of the potential gift. He suggested that they invite the children to a luncheon on campus to discuss their late-mother's intentions. The family attorney extended the invitation and the luncheon was set for the private room at the GSU Faculty Club.

President Larson began the luncheon simply and in

heartfelt fashion. "Before we say anything else, I want you all to know just how much I am truly sorry about your mother's passing. I know what an incredible impact both of your parents have had on this community, and to be honest, am only comforted by knowing that they are now together."

He continued, "Now I think most of you know Jonathon, and that he went to school with a couple of you."

Jonathon quickly added "Eric, Jr. and I went to school together. And I want to say that I'm really sorry about Beatrice's passing as well."

"If you both are so sorry and so sensitive, then why won't you leave us alone about this engineering business," said Steven, one of the children.

Eric, Jr., of whom Jonathon was hoping would support his cause, added "You know, people have been coming after my parents' money for years, and this is just the latest version of 'we want your money.'"

"Now that's not true, Eric, and you know it," Jonathon began assertively. "Both your mom and dad wanted to create an engineering school here. You know that. They've talked about it for years."

"No, the only thing that has been talked about for years is your coming around mom's office looking to get on her good-side and swindle money from her," one of the children said.

"Come on," Jonathon began to get defensive.

President Larson saw the meeting was getting out of hand quickly, as one of the children stood up and began to put on her coat. Steve, angrily, began to stand up as well as he muttered something under his breath about criminal activity. Larson stood up and said, "Please, please, let's not let this get so crazy. We were simply trying to follow up on what we believed was the last wish of your mother."

Two of the children stormed out of the luncheon, as the other two awkwardly sat in silence, trying to decide if they should stay or leave. Jonathon felt betrayed by the children and thought that he should get into a different profession.

Larson did not want to let the possibility of a $50 million gift go, so he consulted with the Board of Trustees about filing a lawsuit against the Reinhold estate. The GSU attorneys believed that they had a good case to get the money away from the children. The Trustees, though, were reluctant to file suit.

The Reinhold family attorney came forward with an offer of $10 million to create a school or college of engineering, in their father's name, provided the University drop all claim to the estate note and the possible $50 million gift.

To Conclude the Discussion

1. What, if anything, could the University have done differently to assure the gift prior to Mrs. Reinhold's vacation? Is Jonathon at fault for not insisting on a legal document before the Alaska trip?
2. What impact did or could the telephone call from the hospital to the attorney have on the legal standing of the gift? Do you think the children should have made the gift to the University?
3. Should the University accept the $10 million gift for a college or school of engineering? What other financial obligation would that incur to the University?
4. What do you advise President Larson to do next? What should Larson say to Jonathon about the gift and the entire situation? Do you encourage him to stay with his job or consider other professions?

5. To what extent is a situation such as this a reflection of a small development staff? Would the situation have the same outcome if there was a larger staff with a dedicated planned giving officer? What do you consider to be the institutional "lessons learned" from this scenario?

Case Study 5:
System and Campus Administration

The California Master Plan of 1960, largely credited to Clark Kerr, created a template for the rise of university systems. In the California Master Plan, specific types of programs and degrees were assigned to community colleges, comprehensive universities, and research universities. This plan further aligned institutions in their academic disciplines. Many other states followed suit, and in the 1970s and 1980s, many states began to formalize systems of higher education. These systems were often created to prevent 'mission-creep' among certain institutions, to enhance efficiency among institutions, and to increase fiscal incentives, such as larger buying power for pensions and medical coverage plans.

In the southwest, the State University System is a large multi-campus system with 12 campuses and over 100,000 students. The diverse system consists of 6 four year institutions, four 2 year community colleges, one upper division university and a stand-alone medical school and hospital in the state capitol. The land-grant university that was incorporated into the system is located in University Park, a typical college town of 100,000 people that includes the 30,000 students enrolled there. The University has a strong national reputation, and the campus houses the majority of the doctoral programs of the system. Four of the other six campuses house professional doctoral degrees, such as the Occupational Therapy Doctorate and the Doctor of Nursing Practice. The State University also, though, houses a research intensive medical center.

The State University Medical Center (SUMC – sometimes called "sumac") is internationally known for its work with liver transplants and research. Although the SUMC has had some public relations problems related to stem-cell research, the Center competes for and receives millions of dollars in research grants each year. The experimental nature of some of the research brings patients to the Center from around the world, and their success in medicine has led to strong fundraising success. The Center has had so much success in fundraising that their endowment is the largest in the State University System and they raise more each year than SU or any other campus.

Not completely unusual, the state system also houses a medical center complex that is a stand-alone academic hospital in the state capitol. The Central State Medical Center has struggled to participate in research, and instead, has focused on patient care and sometimes rural medicine. CSMC also has tried to compete for grants to serve the indigent population of the state's capitol, and while a noble service, has not been able to translate that commitment to financial security. The service model has not helped CSMC financially, and the institution has struggled financially for the past three decades.

CSMC's community clinic, a hallmark of their work with the public, had to begin charging market-rate fees for their work, and as the prices increased, cash flow and revenue began to decrease substantially. Central State's President, Dr. Chris Boes, began to comment publicly that the medical center was in jeopardy of closing. For over five years, he lobbied the state legislature for more resources and eventually turned to the State University System for support. His primary argument was that there is a tremendous need to take care of people who cannot afford to take care of themselves, and this costs money. If CSMC does not have an infusion of cash immediately, "we will have to cease all operations before the end of the academic year and re-direct our medical students to other institutions."

Dr. Boes' comments stirred the public media in the capitol city and around the state. A number of philanthropic organizations committed their "whole hearted" support for CSMC, and a wide number of fundraising dinners and 5K fun runs were pledged to help fund patient care. These activities, however well intentioned, raised only a minimal amount of money. Boes approached several medical supply producers for support, and in politely declining his fundraising efforts, commented that they did not want to support an institution that might be closed or shut down in the near future.

Boes put his budget and accounting team to the task of determining exactly how much money they had, how much they needed, and how much more, long term, would be required for them to maintain their current level of operations. He also started creating plans to close different offices within the Center, possibly closing the community clinic, all research office activities, and just focusing on rehabilitative sciences such as physical therapy and occupational therapy.

As the scenarios were being developed, the accounting staff identified the minimum amount of money necessary to operate through the end of the fiscal year, four months, was $9.3 million dollars. This would cover all obligations of the Center, mostly personnel and facility costs, and would immediately reduce by 50% the operation of the community clinic. Without the cash, the Center's administration would need to begin issuing statements of termination, indicating that state employees would be terminated from their positions due to financial distress. The initial list of employees to be terminated included 47 classified staff members.

Boes did not like the thought of the terminations, and decided to take his budget information directly to ask the State University System President for the money to continue operations. System President Dr. David Wood was well aware of the financial problems at Central State, but was not excited to learn of their ask to be "bailed out."

Let's Pause Here

1. What other financial options might you consider to help CSMC stay in full operation? Are there potential types of donors who might fit well with the scope of their work?
2. Consider that there are two medical schools in the state. How might their cooperation better prevent such a financial crisis?
3. Is there any good that can come from closing CSMC? Come up with a listing of the advantages and disadvantages of supporting two comprehensive medical schools in the same state.
4. Did Boes do the right thing in asking for the system to "bail out" CSMC? Should he have considered this option at an earlier time?
5. If you are System President Wood, what is your response to Boes? How can you think strategically about a response to him and keeping CSMC open?

The State University System Chancellor, Dr. Thomas

"Buzz" Shew, was angered that CSMC had gotten so out of control. He privately blamed Boes, but would not admit that in public. As a system office, he did not have large savings or carry-forward accounts the way that individual campuses sometimes did, but he did have the power of his position. He decided, with only the consultation of his immediate systems-office staff, to create a plan where all of the campuses in the system would give up their savings and carry-forward monies to 'bail-out' CSMC for the current fiscal year. He also thought that he might be able to get some emergency relief funding from the Governor's office. He planned on asking the Governor for $4 million, meaning that the system campuses would need to cover the other $5 million.

The Chancellor issued a memo to each of the individual campus presidents indicating that they would be 'billed' proportionately based on their student enrollment. He intended to brief the campus leaders further in their weekly conference call, but in his memo, indicated that they would be responsible for transferring funds to his office cost centers within one month, and that they could use a combination of their tuition and state appropriations, unrestricted endowment or from unrestricted gift funds, or they could raise gift funds to cover the costs.

The University Park campus, based on size, was assigned a transfer goal of just over $3 million. The President of the flagship campus, Dr. Dorothy Moll, called an emergency meeting of her cabinet to discuss the issue and try to arrive at a solution. Simultaneously she sent a stern e-mail to the system chancellor, objecting to his decision, and arguing that it was very bad precedent to ask one campus to bail out another. She further stated that the gift money he referenced, largely directed at the University Park campus, was given by parents for tuition and fees or by donors for that particular campus only, and using those funds for other campuses, even in the system, was improper at best and possibly illegal at worst. She copied all of the Board of Trustees members on her email message.

Chancellor Shew expected some push-back, especially from those on the University Park campus who typically saw themselves as something of an outsider in the system. The University Park campus was certainly the biggest and most well-known, but it also did not serve the first generation and at-risk students so many of the other campuses did try to take care of. Shew held to his plan, and had the full support of the 10 member Board of Trustees. Shew did recognize that the two student representatives on the Board did not vote in favor of the plan, although he, along with the other Board members, felt that the students could afford to be 'idealists' driven by their emotions rather than the realities of operating a complex university system.

President Moll's objections, while noted by the Board, fell on deaf ears and she was told to "find the funds somehow." Moll called Shew directly following the Board meeting.

"Buzz," she began, "I know things are tight down there at the capitol, but this is just crazy. Because Boes and his team can't put together a decent budget, you are going to bring us all down."

"Dorothy," he responded, "whether you like it or not, you are part of this family. We are a system. A System. And our institutions draw synergy from one another, and the only way we serve our state is by combining our resources to take care of our citizens."

"Seems to me," she commented quickly, "that the citizens you want to take care of are squarely not on this campus!"

The conversations did little to alleviate the growing tension between the System office and the University Park campus. After a full-day retreat on the financial transfer with her senior executive cabinet, Moll decided to try to raise the funds from alumni and friends of University Park. This would be a difficult task, as the flagship was already in a capital fundraising campaign and was finding it difficult to raise significant private funds due to the economic condition of the state and region. And because it was to happen so quickly.

Moll asked her development team to put together an aggressive campaign to raise the funds within 4 months, and she would use accounting to cover the immediate payout to the system. The Vice President for Development expressed her strong feelings that such a task was not likely possible, but accepted as she really had no choice.

Despite the Vice President's positive public attitude that anything is possible, the fundraising volunteers at University Park objected strenuously to the added burden of raising $3 million for another campus, and sent a very strong letter to the campus president and system chancellor expressing their serious objections. They also sent a copy of the letter to the *Daily Mountain*, the state-wide newspaper, making the controversy and campus politics very public.

The chairman of the board of trustees became nervous and angry about negative reports in the media and told President Moll to "find the money from somewhere and stop fighting her boss. Shut it, Moll!" he angrily yelled at her, and concluded with "show a united front or show me your resignation!"

As President Moll was engaged in a very public battle with Chancellor Shew and the Board, the other campuses were struggling to meet their obligations to the system as well. One of the regional colleges, with little flexibility in their budget, canceled all sports programs. Another closed a vocational center for the remainder of the academic year. And yet another transferred all of their savings, an account intended for capital construction renovation, to the system. Even though these campuses had smaller funding targets, they felt a true pain in sacrificing funds.

To very few people's surprise, the development team at University Park was not able to raise the $3 million in private funds for their system payment. President Moll, with few options and an angry board, elected to take make an incremental immediate budget cut on all units on campus to generate the needed $3 million.

Let's Pause Here

1. Does President Moll have a valid point that the payment plan is unfair? If so, how could she have better communicated this to the system's office? Would any different messaging result in a different outcome?
2. From the Board's perspective, is Shew's plan valid? Would it have been better to simply shutter CSMC? What other options might the Board have considered?
3. Could the system campus leaders cooperate to fight Chancellor Shew's plan? If so, what might that have included, and who should be responsible for bringing these individuals together?
4. The development staff was willing to try and raise the $3 million for the system's payment. What kinds of strategies could the development staff use to raise these funds? Who would prospective donors be? What benefit could the development staff communicate to prospective donors regarding the importance of the $3 million campaign?

5. How should Chancellor Shew's office respond to the negativity and discontent among the system campus leaders? Is there a way for Shew to present an image that the financial cost and impact on the other campuses is worthwhile to protect CSMC?

Faculty on the University Park campus were extremely upset at Chancellor Shew's decision to take money from "their" campus. The faculty senate wrote a letter contesting the Chancellor's decision, and called for him to come talk with the faculty. Chancellor Shew declined the offer for a face-to-face meeting, and tensions between the campus and the system escalated to the extent that the faculty contacted the American Association of University Professors to help intervene with the system.

The AAUP referenced best practices and academic freedom and underlying issues with the system behaving inappropriately. The local chapter wrote a letter to the state attorney general seeking a ruling that the taking of money from one government agency to another was inappropriate. The attorney general's office quickly ruled that the university system was in fact one combined university, and that individual campuses did not have the right to disobey the state chartered line of authority.

The AAUP chapter along with the University Park faculty senate wrote a second letter, signed by more than 500 faculty members calling for Shew to change his plan and for the Board to ask for his resignation. A protest at Founders Hall on campus drew several hundred, although President Moll neither publicly endorsed nor condemned the faculty's actions.

Undeterred, Chancellor Shew continued his policy of placing the financial burden on the campuses, and began to realize that even with the immediate infusion of cash, it would take at least another six months of support to bring CSMC into a more stable financial setting. With minimal support from the Governor and the legislature, he would have to increase the financial allocation to be taken from each campus again in the new fiscal year. Several on Shew's staff began to think that the CSMC support was not going to be sustainable and questioned, in private meetings, his approach to "robbing the campuses."

In one explosive conversation among Shew's inner-working group, a vice chancellor commented that the divisive nature of the re-allocation plan was causing such consternation that perhaps they should change course altogether and begin the process of closing CSMC. The unnamed vice chancellor expected an open conversation, but instead, was shut down immediately by Chancellor Shew. Shew bellowed, "we are in this and we are not turning around or giving in to those loud mouth faculty who think they have the right to do whatever the hell they think they want. It's called *academic* freedom, not freedom to do whatever they want!"

In what was becoming a growing media story, a reporter for the *Daily Mountain* interviewed Shew. When asked about the growing unrest of the campuses, Shew commented: "I'm afraid some of our campus leaders are getting faculty worked up. Our job is to behave as a system, not individual campuses. You would lend your brother or sister your allowance, wouldn't you?"

A prominent donor read the story in the Sunday newspaper and called University Park President Moll, distressed. "Dorothy," he began, "you know I love campus and I fully support you 100%, but I don't have any real love or need for that med center down at the capitol." He continued, "I think based on what Shew is doing, I'm going to have to withhold my pledges to your campaign until all of this is sorted out. And actually, I think I should probably not be involved in anything on campus until this gets resolved. There are just too many politics being aired in public right now."

President Moll had five more phone calls to the same effect, draining her pool of potential leadership donors. In total, over $5 million in gifts to the University Park campus were now in jeopardy of not being paid. Some of those gifts offset personnel salaries, meaning that the system's behavior was causing a ripple effect that impacted even more employees.

To compound problems, donors on the other system campuses saw what was happening at University Park and took similar actions. Phones were ringing in presidential offices on almost every system campus with donors changing their plans. Although many of these gifts were significantly smaller, their absence was highly visible. On one of the regional college campuses, the donor's decision to stop payment on a pledge caused the construction of a building of a new residence hall to be halted. The 'ripple' effect there was that the cost to stop construction was compounded by the penalty the university had to pay to the contractor, the future cost of restarting the construction, the loss of revenue from the residence hall not being opened on time, and the difficulty associated with trying to find new places for students to live in the coming fall term.

The faculty were increasingly angry, morale was sinking throughout the system due to the layoffs that resulted in the system's decision to 'raid their coffers,' and on the University Park campus, President Moll's boss, Chancellor Shew, was blaming her for not happily chopping the campus budget to send them a check. Some days, Moll thought, "it is great to be a college president." Today was not one of them.

To Conclude the Discussion

1. What would you advise President Moll to do? What approach should she be taking with her major donors? What message should she be sending to them?
2. Is Chancellor Shew well advised to change his course of actions and close CSMC? What consequences would come from such an action? What consequences would come from Shew changing his plan of billing the campuses to keep CSMC open?
3. What reaction to the funding strategy should President Boes have? Will he ultimately be blamed for not being able to create a balanced budget to keep CSMC open?
4. Create a list of talking points for Chancellor Shew to convince the individual campuses to participate in his taking money from them. Develop a central argument that systems behavior can be a good thing. Develop a central argument that such centralization defeats free-market competition.
5. What is the long-term philanthropic impact of this situation? What active steps could President Moll and her staff immediately begin to try and have something positive come out of the system's behavior?

Case Study 6:
Athletics and Academics

Hawaii State University is a publicly funded institution on the island of Maui. The University has 16,000 students with 60% coming from Hawaii and the remainder from all 50 states and many foreign countries, especially the Pacific Islands. While the University is relatively new compared with other public institutions in the State, it has established itself as a successful alternative to the University of Hawaii campuses. The campus is known for its independent lifestyle of students, has very few residence halls, and offers a very broad range of programs compared to the system campuses. The University has only one doctoral program and the State's only law school, but is especially known for its College of Environmental Sciences (COES) and the School of Oceanography Sciences. The College makes frequent use of the reef system around Maui, and several foreign countries in Asia send groups of students to study at HSU.

HSU, known as The Whalers, has a comprehensive athletic program, playing many of their games against other universities in the Islands. As a smaller NCAA Division I program, the teams participate in the Pacific Coast Conference, comprised of largely what would be considered 'mid-major' athletic programs. Some years, The Whaler athletic programs financially break-even or even make money, but most years they rely on student fees to operate. The biggest expense is football, and the entire athletic budget is either in profit or deficit based on how they do, whether they make a bowl game, or whether they play a Power Five conference opponent. Student attendance across all sports is sporadic, but when The Whalers are winning, they attend in great numbers.

The president of Hawaii State is 63 year old Simon Levine, who has enjoyed a successful presidency for 12 years. He is only the third president of the University and most recently came to HSU from serving as a president in California. Although he misses San Francisco, he loves Maui and draws frequent media attention for his reputation as a world renowned oceanographer. During his presidency, he has guided the university through very difficult financial times, especially during the Great Recession when the state's economy had difficulties. Despite the financial context of the institution, he has been consistently able to move the university forward through his sheer personality and tremendous fundraising prowess. The strength of his personality was highlighted when faculty and staff were furloughed; he furloughed himself more than any other staff member and personally met with faculty and staff who had to go without a paycheck during that period of time.

President Levine is well respected by state legislators who see him as an honorary Hawaiian. They see in him an altruistic individual who has the best interests of the state and the University as his top priority, unlike some of the other campus presidents who have come to Hawaii only to enjoy the lifestyle and then move back to the mainland. Levine is especially well liked by alumni and major donors, and during his travels, he frequently meets with alumni for dinners and on their visit to Maui, are frequently guests in his home. The university typically raises $25-$45 million each year, and these funds are distributed broadly across academic and athletic programs, and Levine is mainly responsible for a $20 million gift from George Wilson who owns a large chain of drug stores in the islands and whose corporation is listed as a Fortune 500 company.

Mr. Wilson is not an alumnus, but loves HSU football and basketball and attends as many of the games as possible. He vacations in Hawaii and owns a large resort home there as well as several acres of farmland on Oahu. Despite his affinity for the university, many in the islands see him as a "howley" or "carpetbagger" who simply makes his money in the islands but has no allegiance to them. His wealth is estimated to be over $4 billion and is Hawaii State University's largest donor by a sizable margin.

With a large vacation home in Maui, Wilson's interest in HSU is purely for entertainment, and for the students and faculty and staff who frequent his stores. He helped HSU finance a pre-season basketball tournament several years ago, and often visits campus in the fall to attend football games. He also attends several away games for the football team when they play on the mainland. He was the benefactor who paid for the football team to charter a private plane for their game in Nevada rather than flying a commercial airline. In return for his support, the football team named its locker room after him, he has been the VIP for the coin-toss on several occasions, and although it might be denied, the university scheduled a game against a team in San Jose, California so that it would be close to Mr. Wilson. He frequently stops by practices, and many players know him by name.

In addition to support for football and basketball, Wilson has made several large gifts to different academic programs. He endowed at $250,000 scholarship for graduate students in the COES and was excited to have lunch with the scholarship recipients. He asked his former business-partner to help support the COES programs, and his friend contributed an additional $50,000 from his personal foundation.

Wilson told President Levine that he wants to do more for the University and even intimated he might do something very, very significant within a couple of years, although he did not specify what 'very, very significant' meant. Levine expected it would be a gift larger than his last gift of $20 million. Wilson is 77 years old, has a wife who is 52, and is also a major benefactor to his alma mater, Cornell, in upstate New York.

Let's Pause Here

1. Write a mission statement for Hawaii State University. From this mission statement, and based on your experience, list four or five major priorities that you would expect from HSU.

2. What is President Levine's responsibility to Mr. Wilson at this point? They speak frequently and consider themselves to be 'friends.' Does that, or should that, influence Levine's thinking about how to direct Wilson's future gift?

3. Discuss the state of the university, in particular, the role of athletics. Should athletics be seen as a central part of the President's priorities? What role should students play in supporting athletics?

4. What kinds of comments do you think that President Levine gets about his affiliation with Mr. Wilson? If Wilson is not well liked or respected on the islands, does his affiliation with him help or hurt the university?

5. If you are advising President Levine, what kinds of thoughts do you discuss with him about Mr. Wilson's comment? Do you suggest that there might be disadvantages to accepting a large gift from Mr. Wilson?

While the faculty respect President Levine, they have not enjoyed the salary increases for three years, due to the state's budget constraints, and some rumblings among faculty are beginning to be heard. The Provost's study of faculty salaries indicated that they are only at 80% of their peer group's average, and the university has lost some very talented faculty to other institutions due to the low salaries, lack of raises, and high cost of living. The State of Hawaii has cut funding to the University for the last four years, claiming that there was too much redundancy among institutions and programs. Levine has been seen as a masterful president, as he has protected faculty salaries and forced cuts in other budget categories. He has also used enrollment increases to protect the university's base operating budget, and his success in fund raising has helped increase the number of scholarships that fund students enrolling at HSU. There have also been some concerns expressed that although enrollment continues to be consistent, US Census data suggest a drop in high school graduates in Hawaii and help the State Bureau of Research to predict an enrollment drop in Hawaiian higher education.

Due to the newer history of HSU, many of the facilities that were built throughout the 1970's are increasingly in need of repair and updating. Some of the local students they have lost in recent years to California schools have been documented to be about how poor the residence hall and student recreation center have become. Levine brought athletics and student affairs together to plan for a new student recreation center, but even with student self-funding through a fee, the center will not open for another five years.

Athletic facilities have their own problems. Although the football and basketball coaches can recruit well and have the beautiful Hawaiian sunset and location to market, their facilities limit who will come to be a Whaler, and more importantly, who will stay. Many of the non-revenue producing sports and particularly women's sports recruit locally and from far-western mainland locations that are relatively easy to fly to and from. In football and basketball, however, the retention and graduation rates for student athletes hovers around 50%.

Recently, the athletics director, Jeff Lytle, told President Levine that they will not be able to continue to compete in the NCAA Division I level if they do not have a major infusion of resources into the athletics physical plant. Lytle believes the cost for the much needed facilities repairs and upgrades to be around $100 million, and he reminded Levine that six years ago when the football team won the Mountain Bowl that athletics made a profit of $7 million and athletic donations were up over $3 million. Lytle's plans include a new basketball practice facility, a new athletic and academic building meant to improve graduation rates and athletes' grade point averages, major improvements to the football stadium and a complete refurbishment of the track and field area. He also points out that the collaborative work with student affairs will keep the cost down and that they will not need a new weight room.

President Levine understands the importance of sports programs to schools like HSU. In fact, he agrees that their athletics programs have helped put HSU on the map and given them a much broader reputation. He often comments that "sports is the only place you can open up almost any newspaper in the country and read about HSU."

"Jeff," Levine told Lytle, "I understand this completely, and I agree with you on many of these fronts, but I'm just not sure we can pay for it. I also don't know if it should be our top priority."

"But, Simon," Lytle responded, "you and I both know that when we are on TV on New Year's Day, not a single person is sitting in the living room around the country asking what our library holdings are in feminist literature. Or who our faculty members are. Or whether a classroom building has a little dirt on it. Come on, you know perfectly well that if you want to increase enrollment, infuse some cash into this place, you've got to invest in sports a little bit."

"Yeah, but Jeff, I've got a legislative session in two months, I've got the Faculty Senate about ready to pass a resolution on faculty salaries, I've got a staff union that is crying for raises, and on top of all that, the roof on the Palms dorm needs to be replaced because of the storm winds from last month."

"I know, I know, I know all of that. But I also know that cash in your pocket solves a lot of problems. You can go ask those folks in Honolulu for money, but you know it's not coming. You've only got a few good bets, and our sports teams are the best of the bunch."

Simon, aware of the tremendous need for facility repair on campus, also held the future of his own academic discipline. He had dreamed for years about a new facility for oceanography and the school that had brought him and national renown to HSU.

Simon was disturbed by his conversation with the athletic director and headed home a little after six. His wife was already home and they were set for a rare dinner together, alone, at home. He sat on the lanai and looked out at the beautiful ocean that he had spent so much of his life studying and living near. Now, he felt like he was facing a true crisis.

Let's Pause Again

1. Think back to the mission statement you wrote. Based on that statement, what should Simon Levine's financial priority be?
2. Write a list of advantages and disadvantages for making athletics a priority. Be sure to think about the scope of HSU as what is often called a "mid-major" athletic program.
3. Discuss the competing priorities for scarce resources and what might be fund raising priorities. How do these look from the perspective of legislators? From students? From faculty? From staff?
4. What arguments could Jeff Lytle use to win over the faculty and staff of the university? How might he do that? What platforms could he use to publicly make his case?
5. How should President Levine start thinking about the fiscal state of the university? Should he be optimistic that the legislature will provide them with money? Should he plan on launching an aggressive fund raising campaign? Should he sign on with athletics?

A new state of the art facility for the School of Oceanography is estimated to cost $45 million. Being an oceanographer himself, President Levine feels a commitment to the school faculty and alumni to build a new facility for the school and has even made promises that it is his highest priority. He knows that most, if not all of the cost will have to come from private gift support. Naturally, Mr. Wilson has been on the top of the list as a possible donor for the building.

Athletics Director Jeff Lytle is also a fundraiser of some renown. He is known for his aggressiveness; he pursues almost anyone who expresses the least bit of interest in assisting athletics. Lytle has solicited several gifts from Mr. Wilson and they have developed a close friendship through the years, including not only traveling to different sporting events together, but also taking personal trips together. The Wilsons and Lytles traveled together to China three years ago for a river cruise, and frequently bike together through a nearby rainforest on the Big Island.

The entire HSU administration attended the funeral of Mrs. Wilson last year, and Jeff even spoke at her funeral. Jeff and his wife spent a week with Mr. Wilson, as they had planned before his wife died, at his home in the Sonoma wine country. Wilson praises Lytle to President Levine every chance he gets and believes him to be the "savior" of HSU athletics.

During one of their social occasions, Lytle expressed to Mr. Wilson that he would like to speak to him about some confidential matters concerning athletics at HSU. The two men subsequently made an appointment to talk at length the first of the month; a formal meeting in Mr. Wilson's business office.

In the meantime, President Levine did some planning of his own. He met with a small group from the Faculty Senate and talked to them at length about morale on campus. Realizing that he needed to invest something in the academic realm soon, and before the legislative session, he asked his development Vice President Jack Marshall, to fast track the planning for a fundraising campaign for the new building for oceanography. The building project had been openly discussed throughout campus, as well as with Board of Trustees' members, but no firm plans had been created and the President was now ready to begin aggressively planning for a fundraising campaign for the new building. His plans were to raise at least half of he amount needed in private gifts, preferably 60%, and then to issue a bond for the remainder. He intended to place a portion of the gifts into an endowment to help with building maintenance. He thought that the maintenance addition was good practice, but he also believes that such a practice would look good to legislators. If he could show the legislators in Honolulu that he was trying to be self-sufficient and not ask them for every little thing, that they might be more likely to appropriate a cost of living raise. He knew it would upset Lytle, but he also knew that he needed to be concerned about campus morale.

Lytle and Wilson talked openly and frequently, especially when Wilson was spending time in Maui. Wilson was spending two weeks in Maui when he stopped by the athletics office one warm and windy afternoon, a week before they were scheduled to meet in Wilson's office. The two men walked onto the football field and Wilson noted the torn up field turf.

"Jeff, you need to get that taken care of. Somebody could get hurt."

Lytle replied, "I know, I know, but we are trying to replace the hurdles for the steeple chase over on the west track."

"Are you serious? Are things really that tight around here that you can't even take care of the football turf? Why didn't you say it was that bad?"

The two men talked at length about the thing that they rarely talked about, the money needed for athletics. They sometimes talked in general terms about such things as the cost of helmets or how much they would make for a particular game. As savvy as Jeff is at fundraising, he was careful with Wilson. They were friends. He was aware of his wealth, and if the was going to ask for something for athletics, he was going to ask big.

Lytle decided his time was now. He had leeway to talk to Wilson, so he knew he could lay it out there for him to fully comprehend. With the tropical breeze blowing in, the two men stood on the football field with empty bleachers and he explained that he needed a minimum of $100 million to fix Whaler athletics. He even said he doubted they could win the conference again unless there was a major influx of resources to help "our team win like they can and should." They talked seriously about the possibility of raising those kinds of funds from alumni and friends and other possible means of support, including bonding capacity.

To add drama to the discussion, Jeff led Wilson into the team dressing room and the hot tub that was shaped like the island of Maui. The jets had been broken in the tub for two years, and it was black with dirt, grime, and mold. Lytle had rehearsed bits and pieces of this talk with Wilson in his head for years, and now he was actually having the conversation.

"Our guys can't even have a soak after practice," Jeff said.

"In my playing days back at Cornell, there was never anything quite like a hot soak after a practice, especially in the cold of upstate New York!" Wilson replied.

"I don't know what we can do," Jeff added, "but I do know that we can't do any of it without your help and leadership."

Wilson then proceeded to tell Lytle that he would like

to see firm plans for what he had in mind and that if he liked them, he would help him by making a significant gift to the athletic program. Lytle went a step further and asked his friend Wilson if he could afford a matching gift for as much as $25 or $50 million. To a rather stunned Lytle, Wilson said his lawyers have been telling him that he needs to get rid of some stock unless he was ready to pay a huge estate tax bill. He had been thinking about giving $50 million to Cornell, and then said that he would consider doing the same for HSU.

After the meeting, Lytle immediately called Vice President for Development Jack Marshall to tell him the good news that Wilson had all but formally pledged $50 million to athletics. Marshall was speechless and extremely upset and asked Lytle who gave him the authority to solicit the university's largest contributor for $50 million. Lytle did not back down and told Marshall that he didn't need anyone's authority and that President Levine was fully briefed and knowledgeable about the capital needs of athletics and that the support would need to come from private gifts. Marshall told Lytle that the president and the university were "saving" Wilson for a gift to build a new facility for the School of Oceanography.

All three gentlemen, President Levine, A. D. Lytle, and V. P. Marshall met in the president's office that evening to try and sort out what had actually happened and where to go from here. While Levine was not happy with Lytle, he chose to focus on the future and not the past and ignore for now whatever mistakes and miscommunication had taken place. They all agreed that the next step was for Levine to talk with Wilson about his true intent.

The next day, Levine and Wilson spoke by telephone as Wilson had already left for the mainland. While always polite and supportive, Wilson told Levine the following:

"Well, Simon, you know I am a very close friend of your AD. I also feel very close to you and have a great respect for your leadership and judgement. I will indeed make a gift to HSU of $50 million, and no more, but you and the board must decide where to put the gift, academics or athletics. I love both and see both sides of it. You are the president of this place and I think that it is ultimately your responsibility. I only hope we can all be friends after this gets decided!"

To Conclude the Discussion

1. Should the President ultimately decide the gift should go to academics and use to build a new Oceanography building?
2. Since the gift was first asked to be used for athletics, should the president follow that direction?
3. Does the leadership of the faculty have a role in this discussion?
4. Should the Board of Trustees decide the use of the gift and take it out of the hands of the president?
5. What should happen next? If the President directs the money to athletics, what does he tell his faculty colleagues? If he directs it to Oceanography, what does he do about athletics? How does either scenario get conveyed to the legislature to help HSU's case for more state allocations?

Case Study 7:
Perils of Life Insurance Gifts

Stanton State University is a large public comprehensive institution with a student enrollment of 20,000. Located in the lush, fertile farmland of the western United States, it sits in a rural area surrounded by wineries, vegetable farms, mountains to the north, and the beach just two hours to the west. The University attracts students from across the country and many foreign countries, partially due to its proximity to several large west-coast cities. For many years it has been known for its very successful athletics programs, with 12 men's and women's sports. Former Super Bowl coach Jon Rilston got his start at SSU, and is a prominent figure in many discussions of SSU's athletic programs.

Rilston was hired at SSU as a Special Assistant to the Athletic Director to try and rekindle the excitement for athletics on campus. Rilston, over 80 years old now, still has some strong name recognition and connects regularly with many former athletes from mostly basketball and football. One of the most common themes Rilston has heard, and conveyed, is that the athletic facilities have fallen behind many of their peers, and such need hurts recruiting, fund raising, admissions, the public image of the institution, etc. Rilston has been told, and generally agrees, that the university is in need of a new football stadium, basketball arena, track and field venue as well as improvements to other sports facilities, both men's and women's. The university resisted the implementation of a student athletic fee for many years, but recently found the need for such a fee when the economy was not strong and an athletics budget deficit was projected. The fee was not popular among students, and even after it was implemented, the capital construction need was still significant. Implementing a fee and then raising it quickly was not something the administration had an interest in pursuing.

Capital concerns on campus were not limited to athletic facilities, and indeed the entire campus has struggled to maintain an improvement and renovation plan that effectively keeps all academic and non-academic buildings appropriately maintained. Until the past decade, SSU has invested very little in development efforts, and the small endowment for the university reflects that lack of attention. A major emphasis of the president and board is to increase fundraising efforts to develop endowments that can support the institution for generations to come.

The institution's lack of attention to development had not been a problem for past presidents, but had been more of an 'after-thought.' With decent enrollment increases, tuition monies allowed SSU some flexibility in spending, and state revenues had been stable, allowing for past presidents to focus on several initiatives, such as expanding academic programs that responded to local interests and strengths. The implementation of the tourism program and wine-making masters degree were both new and highly desirable degree programs.

With Rilston working to help in any way he can, he developed a strong relationship with a former football player and All-American, Jere "Bull" Smith. Smith played in the NFL for a decade, earning enough money to buy his way into the oil and energy business, and has talked for years about returning Stanton State athletics to their glory days. He has been a consistent, although not significantly large donor, and visits with institutional leaders and those in athletics on a regular basis. He frequently shows up on lists of famous alumni from SSU, is on several advisory boards, and even has an office area in the athletic building that while officially is for visiting personnel, is used primarily by Bull. With a conservatively estimated wealth of $5 billion, SSU pays close attention to his actions and desires.

Bull recently sold his small chain of steak houses and told Rilston and the SSU president that he wants to pledge $100 million to the University for athletics facilities (football first, of course) and wants to challenge other alumni and friends to match his gift. His idea was to pledge $100 million of his own money, and working through athletics, to challenge former athletes to double that amount. Rilston and the athletic department personnel were thrilled to hear this news, and while excited, somewhat cautious and surprised. "The Bull" had been around Stanton athletics so much and had given so little to date, there was some skepticism that he would actually fund his pledge.

"Bull, are you sure you can do this?" Rilston asked one afternoon in the athletics office.

"Jon," he responded, "it's time we get off our butts and do something. Remember those days when the stands were filled? Remember the fall afternoons when those teams from UCLA and USC would visit and we would kick them back down the interstate? Remember that? Well hell, nobody around here is doing anything to bring those days back, and it's up to you and me."

Rilston knew Bull had a point, and also knew that it was easy to talk about restoring sports 'glory,' but quite something different to see it happen. So much had changed in college sports in the past 50 years. Increased competition, increased recruiting costs, increased coaching costs, expanding coaching staffs, greater expectations from students about the amenities available to them. Rilston thought that a $200 million fundraising campaign, with the leadership gift from Bull would be about right. There was so much left to chance, but with that kind of fundraising success, Stanton State might really be on the right track for a return to glory. This could be Rilston's last great final contribution to Stanton, and he was planning on making a gift of his own, perhaps as much as a million dollars saved from his professional coaching days.

Working with the athletics Director of Development, Rilston began to write up plans for what $200 million would do for athletics. Stadium renovations, locker room renovations, major changes to the seating in the basketball arena, and scholarship endowments. The entire athletics department began to feel the excitement of what the infusion of resources could do for them, and the excitement was contagious. Bull walked through the athletic department as a hero.

Let's Pause Here

1. Is the relationship that Bull has with athletics appropriate? Should it be a practice to allow a former student athlete and potential donor to have such complete access to those working in athletics to the extent that he has open access to an office?
2. What would be an effective development strategy for using Jon Rilston as a former famous athletics figure? How would you use his relationship with former athletes?

3. Should Bull have the right to dictate a fundraising campaign? Is he the most appropriate person to establish a fundraising goal? How would you, as the Director of Athletic Development, work with Bull?
4. Is there any institutional concern for pursuing athletic development goals separate or independent of other institutional fundraising goals? Should there be a conversation between athletics and others on campus about prioritizing development goals? If so, who has the responsibility for initiating that conversation? What are the most desirable outcomes for creating conversations among units on campus?
5. How does the athletics department proceed? Bull has a history of involvement, but not a strong history of making gifts. Is it important to get his commitment prior to reaching out to others and formalizing the development campaign?

Bull Smith has been generous to his alma mater, frequently hosting events at his restaurants and making a series of gifts in the $5,000-$10,000 range. Without a large donor base of significant donors, Bull is considered one of the top prospects. His total wealth has also been a primary motivation to allow him access to decision-making in athletics. He has been very involved in all aspect of athletics on campus, and was a key figure in the last search for an athletics director. Many even perceived that he chose the athletic director, and many faculty members question the involvement of him as a donor in decision-making.

Bull's involvement is problematic for the athletics staff as well. As a very wealthy individual he does not have to being concerned with being in an office of one of his enterprises or businesses on a daily basis, so he will often "swoop into the athletics office and be present for a week, commanding everyone about him to do his bidding," as one faculty member commented. Another faculty member, a long-time professor of education commented, "Smith is SSU athletics and nothing is done without his approval."

The perception of Bull in the last athletic director search was not inaccurate. He made phone calls soliciting applications, checked references informally, and even had one of his private airplanes bring his top candidate to campus to interview. The university could have challenged Bull on his involvement, but there was too much collective interest in his financial ability to support the university and athletics. The new athletics director is determined to keep Bull happy, realizing that he partially owes his job to Bull, but also that he could provide many millions of dollars to Stanton athletics.

Despite his professional football career, Bull is in excellent physical shape. He recently had his annual physical and the doctor told him that he was in top physical condition, prompting Bull to purchase a sizable life insurance policy. The policy had a relatively low cost due to his health report. This surprisingly low rate got Bull thinking about his friends from the world of sports, particularly SSU alumni, and whether it would be possible to use life insurance benefits to help the athletic program.

Bull devised a plan where he would get a number of alumni to take out life insurance policies and designate the athletics program at the University as the beneficiary of the policies. He believed that such a program could have huge benefits for the University and even projected that it could raise as much as $250 million for athletics over time. Additionally, he thought that such a pool of prospective life insurance money could be used to leverage good bond ratings and immediate construction could begin.

Bull had no background in the insurance industry and

relied on the insurance brokers he purchased his policy from to advise him and react to his idea to benefit the University. The plan was to get as many as 30 to 50 healthy alumni to each take out a $10 million life insurance policy naming the university athletics program as beneficiary. The premiums would be paid for by the University.

Bull's thinking was that if he had enough alumni sign up for the $10 million policies, that statistically they would start dying within the third year which would more than adequately pay back the premiums. While no one can predict when death will occur, Bull thought that he had devised a full proof plan which, based on statistics, would pay off in a reasonable period of time. Bull even decided to loan funds to athletics to be used to fund the initial premium payments so that the university would not be out any advance funding. Bull would be paid back when the policies started maturing (when the insured started dying).

Bull first unveiled his plan to his good friend Rilston. Rilston, himself in excellent shape and aware of his mortality, thought it was an excellent idea, and even said, "this is fantastic. Let's do it. Let's get this ball rolling!"

The two met with the athletic director who had some apprehensions and did a little bit of online research on his own. Apparently, there was some historical precedence for such a fundraising plan. In the 1980's there were investors who literally bought, at a discount, paid up life insurance policies from victims of Acquired Immune Deficiency Syndrome (AIDS) and cashed them when the AIDS victims died. As morbid as the practice was, the scheme made some investors rich due to the assured death of AIDS victims.

The athletic development team reluctantly agreed to the plan primarily not to offend Bull and Rilston. Privately, they hoped the plan would fail and that Bull would feel compelled to just make an outright cash gift. The development team created a targeted campaign to be delivered to 150 former student athletes who had been identified by Rilston and Bull. The campaign materials included a cover letter from Bull and the athletics director, artists renderings of the newly renovated facilities, and instructions on how proceed with the life insurance gift.

Of the 150 names, 32 former student athletes agreed to take out a $10 million life insurance policy and name Stanton State as beneficiary. The premiums were to be paid by the athletics department and Bull made a cash "loan" to athletics to insure that the first year of premiums would be paid by him and not the University.

Let's Pause Again

1. What is the motivation of Bull to be so engaged in athletics? Does he really have the best interests of the university and Stanton athletics at heart, or could he have some different motive?
2. Could the athletics department do anything different in its handling of Bull? Is it wise to have a donor so engaged in athletics or any academic program? Can or should the university change its relationship with him, and if so, how would that happen?
3. What concerns would you have about the insurance plan as a process to raise money? If you were asked to develop a list of pro's and con's of the plan, what would be on your list?
4. If you had a targeted list of 150 development prospects, what strategies might you use to approach them? What questions would you be asking them about supporting athletics, and how could you use nominal techniques to understand them better?

5. To what extent should university leaders outside of athletics be involved in making a decision to proceed with a plan such as the life insurance fundraiser? To what extent should athletics be considered independent or integrated with the larger university community?

The athletics development staff were enthused by the 32 former student athletes who enrolled in the program; a higher number than they had expected from the onset of the program. Bull financed the entire first year of the premium payments, but the division of athletics had to pay the second year of premiums, just under $5 million. The premium payments were significant because of the age of most of the participants, and this left the staff in the office feeling uneasy. The office joke became that they were on 'death watch,' and bad colds and hospital stays were followed with great interest by those vested in the program's success.

The problem the athletics staff found after the first year, was that the 32 former student athletes were actually in good health. None of the participants died in the first three years of the program, meaning that the university had to pay $10 million to keep the program operating. The fourth year of the program, there was speculation that one person would pass away, but he survived and athletics again paid out another year of premiums, now having invested $15 million and owing another $5 back to Bull for his financing of the first year.

One element that Rilston and Bull did not realize was that these former athletes were still healthy and their habits of jogging, water aerobics, healthy eating, etc., were lengthening their lives. In the fifth year of the program, the athletics department had to turn to the university to help pay the premiums, as they had paid the previous year's premiums by withdrawing money from their endowment principal. The university leadership provided partial support for one year, but refused to extend cash to athletics for further payment. The division of athletics' only option was to continue drawing down on their endowment principal and ultimately decided that they would cut their losses and default on the insurance premiums.

Bull began to change his perception of the program, realizing that instead of raising over $250 million, he had cost the athletics department he loved so dearly millions of dollars and jeopardized endowed scholarships. Although he felt badly about this, he made no initial efforts to resolve the problem.

The insurance company noticed that the athletics department did not pay their premiums on the 32 life insurance policies. The company hired a legal team and filed a motion in federal court to make the athletics department pay the past due premiums and because of their failure to pay, requested a one-year future payment. The court ruled that the university, not just the athletic department, was liable for the past due premiums and that they would have to follow the formal rules to discontinue the policies if that is what they decided to do. The total cost for insurance premium past due payments and future payments for joint cancelation of the policies was valued at $10.1 million by the court. The university would be eligible to collect on any policies that were realized during this time.

The athletics director had few options in obtaining the money for the legal case decision. He made the first, very difficult decision, to eliminate Jon Rilston's position as special assistant to the athletic director. He had a candid conversation with Rilston, expressing extreme appreciation for this past work, but finally said "Jon, this insurance policy plan was just not a good thing for us to get into. The campus is going to loan us some of the money to cover the costs of what we have gotten into, but we've got to cover the rest, just over another $5 million. I never should have allowed us to get into this thing."

Rilston had no good response other than his extreme desire to assist the athletic program he loved so dearly. The athletic director concluded their conversation by saying, "Jon, we are extremely grateful for everything you have done for us, but based on what has happened with Bull and this insurance plan, we are not going to renew your contract when it expires at the end of the calendar year."

Bull was infuriated by the termination of Rilston and even more furious that the athletic department had pinned his termination on the insurance fundraising plan. Bull demanded to speak to the university president, previously an easy request, and he was shocked when the president's secretary indicated that it would be "at least two weeks" before he could be fit onto the president's schedule.

Bull had a moment of extreme anger, and stormed into the athletic offices. The desk where he often held court was covered in boxes and other office supplies, apparently turned into a storage area. The office staff were also decidedly cool toward him and unsure of how to even speak to him. Bull looked around frantically and walked into the athletic director's office.

Bull stood in front of the athletic director's desk, unsure what to say or do, but angry for falling so far from the good graces of the athletics program. He started to speak loudly, but then quieted his voice and said, "I'm, well, I'm sorry. I never wanted this to happen, I only wanted to help. This all seemed like such a good idea when we started."

The athletic director as a compassionate person sat and talked with Bull for a long time, addressing his involvement in athletics, how he had been perceived by faculty and the president's leadership team, and indeed confirmed that Rilston was not being retained because of the poor judgement shown on the life insurance plan.

Bull surprised the athletic director with his next comment. "I'll pay for it. I'll pay for it all. We'll cancel the policies unless some of the guys want to take on their own payment plan for the premiums, but for everyone else, I'll pay for it. You don't have to take any money from campus, just get the figure of what I owe you."

The athletics director wanted to jump for joy, but instead, looked seriously at Bull and said "that would be most welcome around here." He rose and gave him a firm handshake and spoke for a few minutes about a fall football game. As Bull began walking out the door, he turned and said, "I'll get you that check within the week. And, John's got his job back, right?"

To Conclude the Discussion

1. What does the athletic director do about Bull's request to retain John Rilston? Should the athletic director ask for anything additional from Bull?

2. Did the president of the university and the Board of Trustees have an obligation to review the life insurance scheme very closely and insure that it made good sense? Should the board of trustees have called in insurance experts to review the scheme and advise the board on the appropriateness of the project?

3. Did the athletics director and Jon Rilston become too close to Smith, clouding their judgement in allowing the program to move forward?

4. Was the whole program basically a sham or gamble from the very beginning where the athletics department was simply betting folks would die prematurely?

5. Should donors be allowed to influence university programs simply because personnel are afraid to upset them and risk the loss of gifts?

Case Study 8:
White Elephants and Gifts That Eat

North Boston University is a prestigious private institution of approximately 14,000 students affiliated with the Quakers, Religious Society of Friends. NBU was founded in 1798 and has a proud history of offering a liberal arts education to a diverse student body.

While it remains a well-known and moderately selective institution, it has seen a slight drop in enrollment over the last 10 years. The faculty are adamantly opposed to lowering admissions standards to increase enrollment and the decline in student numbers has caused a concomitant strain on the annual budget. In fact, for the first time since the depression, the university is projecting a slight deficit in the coming fiscal year. The Board of Curators is understandably concerned about the deficit and decline in enrollment.

The president of North Boston University, Dr. Xavier Dolling, is in his second year as head of the institution and followed a highly successful president with a 22 year tenure. Following such a long-term president, many are still undecided about the new president. Many university constituents, faculty, alumni, students, as well as community-minded Bostonians are watching him closely to see if he is up to the job.

To further complicate matters, Dr. Dolling is not a

member of the Society of Friends, although he is a Protestant. In recent years the University has moved further away from Society of Friends affiliation and the Board of Curators felt it was time to consider someone outside the church as the CEO, a decision that was met with some controversy.

The decline in enrollment has placed an added strain on the fundraising efforts, particularly the annual fund which supplements the overall budget to maintain budget equilibrium. The new president has also called on the development office to raise more funds for scholarships to assist the decline in enrollment.

The Vice President for University Advancement, Ross Hallowell, is a well-regarded fundraiser with almost 40 years of experience in development. He has built a solid fundraising program at NBU and is highly recognized and respected for his expertise. He has brought in several multimillion dollar gifts to the University during his tenure, and has been at the university for most of his career. At 65 years old, and while vigorous and in good health, he has started considering retirement, especially after the former president, who was a close personal friend of his stepped down. Hallowell has confided in a few curators that life is very different under the new president and that there is a "lot of nervousness" among staff and faculty with the change of leadership.

Vice President Hallowell has been cultivating a former curator for many years, and is very close to bringing in the largest gift in the University's history. The potential donor, Maxfield Robertson, is a Quaker and a graduate of NBU, class of 1948. He is 90 years old and in poor health. He owned a profitable ball bearing company in Boston that his grandfather founded. He sold the company for an undisclosed amount, but local rumors indicate that it was for over $40 million dollars. Robertson is married with no children. His wife, Mabel, is also a Quaker and very involved in the Society of Friends. She is a graduate of Swarthmore College in Philadelphia and comes from an old Philadelphia, "high-society" family.

Maxfield Robertson has decided to give his home and surrounding grounds to NBU. His home consists of over 20 acres of prime Boston residential real estate with an appraised value of $25 million. Robertson has planted over 10,000 azaleas on the property and it is a spectacular, manicured setting. People come from around the state and region to see his azaleas when in bloom.

The grounds also have a large 18th century manor house filled with beautiful antiques. There are two smaller houses on the property that were used as residential servant's quarters, but now mostly serve as coordinating areas for staff who live off-site. The Robertson home is one of the most beautiful homes and settings in Boston proper.

Robertson has committed to give the property, along with an endowment of $5 million for the maintenance and upkeep of the property, as long as the University uses the property as an arboretum. The University is to keep the estate in perpetuity and use it as an outdoor classroom and research venue for students and faculty. The house is to be used as either guest quarters for university visitors, or, perhaps as a residential college for students studying landscape architecture.

Vice President Hallowell tried to delicately explain to Robertson that such a gift, while very, very generous, could someday become a burden on the institution and cost huge sums in maintenance and upkeep. Hallowell told Robertson that a $5 million endowment might not be sufficient to maintain the property much less provide academic funds for students and faculty.

Hallowell had very mixed feelings about the gift. On the one hand he very much wanted to accept it as he felt the Robertson's might give more in the future, although they did recently make a sizeable gift to Mabel's alma mater, Swarthmore. On the other hand, he was worried about placing restrictions on the use of the property that could become a burden on the University in the future. He also felt, as he explained to the donor, that a $5 million endowment was woefully inadequate for the maintenance of the property.

On top of those concerns, the University did not even have a landscape architecture program in its curriculum. The closest thing to an academic program that might fit with the use of the property from an academic standpoint was a program in botany, a stretch to say the least. And, yet another concern was the distance from the campus, 30 miles to the north, and a busy, high traffic commute. The idea of a guest house for University visitors was totally unrealistic due to this distance.

President Dolling, however, was quite insistent that they find a way to accept the property as it would be a significant event in the life of the institution and his administration. He applied considerable pressure to his vice president to "make it happen."

Let's Pause Here

1. Develop a transition plan for President Dolling upon entering the NBU presidency? Specifically, how can he best introduce himself to key university constituents.
2. Write a list of pro's and con's for NBU to accept the gift. Based on the list you develop, would you advocate for or against accepting the property?

3. If you are President Dolling, what do you expect from Vice President Hallowell? How could Dolling best use Hallowell, and how would this use impact Hallowell's ideas about how the university is being run?
4. Thinking strategically about the property gift, are there any ways you can think of to use it as leverage for other gifts? What other revenue streams, public and private, might be tied to the university taking ownership of a grand estate such as this?
5. Should the Robertson gift to Swathmore concern the NBU development staff? How can learning about this gift be used constructively for NBU?

Hallowell continued confidential conversations with Robertson over a lengthy period of time in the hope of convincing him to relax the restrictions on the property so that the university would be comfortable in accepting it. "We really, truly want to make your estate a major part of who we are and what we can do, but without some flexibility for 50 years from now, we just can't take the risk of the property," Hallowell had said.

Hallowell continued the cultivation of Robertson, and met with him almost monthly for lunch, coffee, dinners, and drinks, and the property was always prominent in their conversations. After two years of back and forth negotiations and serious discussions, Robertson's health began to deteriorate. Doctors discovered a fast moving cancer in Robertson and told him he should "begin to get his affairs in order."

Within a week of finding out this bad news, Robertson called Hallowell and asked him to come visit him as soon as was convenient. Hallowell came to his home the next day. Robertson confided in Hallowell that his health was declining and he wanted to get his affairs in order, which included the disposition of his property. He said that he had been thinking it over and now understood that it would not be proper to hinder future generations with restrictions on the property. He had concluded that he would give the property with a provision that it be used as an arboretum, but, that if that use was no longer feasible in the future, the property could be sold and the funds used for academic purposes at the University.

Hallowell thanked Robertson and promised to put university attorneys with Robertson's attorneys to create appropriate documents as soon as possible. Time was of the essence as Robertson's health continued to deteriorate.

The documents included a clause that Mabel Robertson could continue live on the property, and in the main residence for her lifetime, as long as she paid $10,000 a month rent to the University. Maxfield felt very strongly that after he was gone, Mabel should move to an assisted living care facility and not attempt to maintain such a large estate. He placed the rent provision in the document to encourage her to leave the property after his death. Mabel was extremely upset with this provision.

When it came time to sign the documents, Mabel objected to the rent provision and refused to sign. The couple argued bitterly, as this was Mabel's home as well as Maxfield's, and the two had built their entire life in the house. They had held spring parties, supported politicians, and even hosted foreign dignitaries in these hallways and rooms. The house had been decorated in Mabel's preferred style, and seeing her husband try and "force" her out, broke her heart even more as she watched Maxfield deteriorate as the cancer ate away at him.

Late one night, as Maxfield moved closer to death, he looked at his dear wife with tears in his eyes, and she knew that she must do anything to help him feel at ease. Without saying a word to him the next morning, she phoned the attorneys and signed away her rights to the home, but not the furniture and interior property. She was able to smile and hold Maxfield's hand as he died, with him knowing that she had fulfilled his wishes. The property that she had loved so dearly would transfer to the University, and she would have to begin paying rent on "her" house.

President Dolling along with Vice President Hallowell were present at Maxfield's funeral, and they were certain to have a large floral wreath sent from the University. Several other University offices had flowers sent as well, and NBU was well represented at the graveside burial. Mabel had mourned for her husband and would miss every aspect of his life being intertwined with hers, but she was able to look coldly at "the vultures" from the University. She was gracious as she accepted their condolences, and Dolling and Hallowell thought only of her grief as an excuse for her coldness.

The day after the funeral, she phoned her personal attorneys and had them take over the affairs of herself and Maxfield's estate. The move was met with some suspicion by Maxfield's attorney who had been with him for over 50 years. "Mabel, this is a coup! You are making a huge mistake. You are just in grief, give things a few days or weeks, and then let's talk. You've got everything you could want here. Just let me do my job," Maxfield's attorney had said.

"I don't have everything I want, and it has been very clear to me for some time that all you were successful at doing was encouraging an old, dying man's fantasies," Mabel responded. "You were a faithful friend to Maxwell, and for that I am thankful, but I must concern myself with my own affairs from this day forward," and she hung up.

Working through her attorney, she immediately contacted NBU and asked for a one-year grace period before she would have to begin paying the $10,000 a month rent. Her argument was that the University would be getting the estate soon enough, and that she, in her grief and transition, just needed a little time to get her affairs in order and figure out her finances. Hallowell and Dolling had no real concerns about this delay, and consented through their legal counsel almost immediately. They had scarcely noticed the change in attorneys contacting their own lawyers.

"Part of the reason I don't mind," Hallowell had said, "is that I feel badly for the old lady. Max sure took care of her, and I don't know if I would have signed."

"Let's just be forever thankful that she did," Dolling responded. "That old place up there is worth a fortune to us. I think we can probably sell off half of it after Mabel passes away, and that will certainly give us some momentum to move forward." Dolling's thought had not been discussed before, but it did not shock Hallowell. He had observed how Dolling had been working with the faculty and the board, and his transition to the presidency had been somewhat unstable. He had some successes with student enrollment increasing, but he had not made the in-roads many thought he would be able to in fundraising and budget stabilization.

Let's Pause Again

1. If Dolling's intention is to sell the property, should he have been more forthright with Hallowell and Maxfield? If that was his intention all along, is there a way that it could have been honestly communicated to Maxfield with the same result?
2. What are the stewardship responsibilities for both

Dolling and Hallowell in working with Mabel? Should her lack of compassion with them be seen as something more than her grieving? Should they have followed up when she did not warmly receive them?

3. As an institution, is there a possibility to "over-do it" when it comes to stewardship? Should there have been so many floral arrangements from NBU? Should these have been more stringently coordinated, or did the overflow of flowers make it appear that NBU was very saddened by Maxwell's death? Or, did it make it look like NBU was over compensating for their desire for their money?

4. With the revelation of Dolling, does Hallowell have any responsibility to Mabel at this point in time? What ethical questions might he be debating in his mind, and what actions might arise from these? What responsibility does he have for the memory of Maxfield?

5. What should NBU's strategy be for the estate and property? Would selling it off in pieces to raise capital be the approach you would recommend? Would preserving it add a different dimension to the University and its cultural and academic life?

A year to the day after Maxfield's death, the University attorney's worked with their financial investment firm to arrange for a billing and payment procedure, specifically an automated payment for rent from one of Mabel's many accounts. No one anticipated any difficulty until the investment firm informed them that Mabel would be responsible for paying the taxes on the benefit of living rent free in "her own home." The value of rent, $10,000 a month, was expanded over the past year, and she owed back taxes on $120,000 of an "income equivalent" benefit.

So in addition to her first month of rent, she would owe approximately $34,000 in back taxes.

The taxation issue angered Mabel more than hurt her financially; such a sum of money was nothing to her other than perhaps her annual tennis bill. She was furious, though, that the University had failed to project such an income tax issue; just more poor management by NBU, trying to "suck dollars from my dry bones!" She set an immediate meeting with her attorneys.

"I want to buy my home back," she told them. "This is my home, and I shan't leave it. Maxfield, God rest his soul, made me sign it away, and I have no intention of leaving. Let's offer those blood-suckers fifty percent of the value of the home or take them to court. I can't imagine that Dolling and his droll little team will bat an eye. They should be happy to get anything, I should think."

Mabel's attorney's contracted with a specialized law firm in Philadelphia, and they offered a price of $12.5 million for the estate and grounds, and in doing so, would qualify for a tax deduction of another $7 million. All agreed that this was fair, as the University would receive $12.5 million dollars for doing nothing other than signing a paper. If they had more than greed in their hearts, she thought, they would accept the offer and leave her alone.

Hallowell was more conflicted than ever, and closer to walking away from his job after over 40 years at NBU. He was concerned about Dolling's intentions with the property, but was also deeply concerned about not using the property for an arboretum, which is what Maxfield had originally intended. He had spent more time with him than anyone, perhaps even his wife, in the years preceding his death. Selling the property to Mabel was just like selling to anyone else as it violated the trust that Maxfield had in him. But, not selling the property to her would most likely result in Dolling pushing the breaking up and sale of the property to someone outside of Maxfield's family. He was feeling that he was in a no-win situation. Hallowell made his feelings known to Dolling who looked at him as an 'idealist' rather than strategic development officer.

"I know you were close to Max," Dolling had said. "The plain reality of the situation, though, is that this place has taken up far too much of our time already, and we can get some much needed cash in our pockets if we sell it off. Now, if you think we can sell it in a year or two and double what we can bring in, then don't sell it to Mablel. If the old girl is going to be around for a while, I think we should probably take the money now."

After hearing Hallowell's opinion that Mabel would be around for another five or ten years, Dolling was very much in favor of selling the property to her and using the funds for student scholarships. As an "outsider" of the Quaker faith, he was not having much success in raising money for the institution, as he was failing to connect with the most affluent giving prospects. He was making good progress modernizing the internal operations of the institution, and the Board of Curators were grateful to him for that, but he needed cash to keep moving the institution forward.

The attorneys for both parties met privately to discuss all concerns related to the proposed purchase of the estate and grounds. Dolling had taken an informal poll of the Board of Curators, speaking to each one individually, and had their permission to proceed with the sale. The lone condition they set was that they could keep the $5 million endowment that had been intended to maintain the estate and grounds. Mabel's attorneys agreed to the endowment staying with NBU as long as it would be for scholarships that included Maxfield's name, and that the

University pay her $34,000 in back taxes. All attorneys agreed to the deal and prepared the appropriate paperwork for final signature.

Dolling sat in the Board room of the administration building to sign the paperwork, along with the Board of Curators chairman, the NBU attorneys, and Hallowell. Dolling signed the papers on all of the pages identified by the attorneys, and passed them to the Board chair.

"Wait," said Hallowell, breaking the silence of the room. "I know you have all agreed to this, but I have to speak my mind."

"A little late for that," Dolling sharply retorted.

"No, I don't think it is," Hallowell continued. "Maxfield was a good man who cared deeply about NBU, his wife, and a whole lot of charities throughout Boston. He gave throughout his entire life, and he was exacting, never making a gift without serious consideration and a full understanding of what he was giving to. I knew Max for over 25 years, and in the last five years of his life, I met with him probably more than anybody else, except maybe for his personal staff. Max was a friend. He was a friend of NBU. He was a loyal husband, and he expressly did not want what you are about to sign. He wanted his wife taken care of. He wanted his estate to live on, celebrating his life and work and the beauty that can be Boston. If you sign those papers Mr. Chairman, you are taking that away from his memory. I beg you, I beg you not to do this."

Dolling and the chairman looked at each other. They looked at Hallowell, a long time, trusted colleague and defender of NBU. The chairman of the Board held his pen firmly, looked again at Dolling, and signed the legal agreement selling the property to Mabel.

To Conclude the Discussion

1. Should the University leadership be concerned that Maxfield's wishes to have an arboretum were not met? What does Hallowell do now?
2. Should President Dolling and Vice President Hallowell have discouraged acceptance of the gift, knowing they would never fulfill the donor's wishes of an arboretum? Should North Boston University have advised Maxfield Robertson to make his gift to a different institution that had a landscape architecture program and that could fulfill his stated goal?
3. Should Hallowell have encouraged and even insisted that Mable be taken care of and not have to pay monthly rent? Could Hallowell have addressed his job differently in this process?
4. Did university officials adequately represent Mabel's interests, given she was the donor as well? What is the responsibility of NBU to "steward" Mabel moving forward?
5. Could this gift transaction have spiraled out of control and become a public relations nightmare? How might such be prevented? Does this entire gift transaction leave a bitter taste or is it just part of the business of philanthropy?

Case Study 9:

Beware of Arbitrage

Johnson State University is a Midwestern, regional public institution of approximately 10,000 students. The institution has maintained it's enrollment over the last 10 years and is known as a great value and excellent education, especially for a comprehensive university. The faculty generally are retained at high rates, and when hiring occurs, they are typically capable of landing their top prospects. Undergraduates are mostly in-state students, and the small town environment of JSU has the look and feel of a very traditional "college town." The one area that JSU struggles with is the physical facilities on campus. The "old quad" and "campus pond" help draw students to campus, but increasingly, poor residential hall facilities and classroom facilities are becoming a problem. The Provost even noted that when three faculty left the previous year for other, peer-institutions, the comments he heard were about office space, library facilities, and the lack of technology in classrooms were all issues.

The primary issue that JSU was facing was that state dollars had been constant, and that these funds did not allow for any capital improvement or expansion. In terms of facilities, the university was "treading water." The university did get some relief from the state historical society for a renovation of the Old Main building, but that ended up causing even more conflict, as it appeared that the administrative offices were refurbished rather than taking care of students and faculty. JSU was not alone, however, as none of the state institutions were receiving funds for academic building renovation.

The president of Johnson State University is relatively new to her position. She has a fundraising background and is known for being quite progressive and forward thinking. President Gloria Havilland has been at JSU for six months and has been in an intensive strategic planning effort since the first day she arrived on campus. She was very familiar with JSU when she arrived on campus, and knew that she would have to focus on facilities immediately, and that all other issues, from student recruitment to technology in the classroom would stem from what she did in this regard. As a person who typically worked on a 'fast-track,' she knew this would have to be faster.

Before she arrived on campus, President Havilland met with each Board of Trustee member and asked for a list of what they individually considered the campuses biggest critical issues. Each Trustee had the campus' physical facilities as a top three priority. She then met with each of the vice presidents and the president of the Faculty Senate, and again, facilities were on all of their lists as a primary concern. She felt validated about her perceptions of campus before she even started her job: fixing facilities was clearly job number one.

By the time President Havilland started her job, she had a rough idea of how she could begin prioritizing the needed construction and how to pay for it. Her next step was to meet with local legislators to affirm her guess that there would be no additional state money coming forward. Next, she worked through her Provost to assign each academic dean and functional area the task of assessing their facility needs. She wanted them to start affixing dollar values to the needed repairs, not just abstract comments about needing new classrooms or offices. Campus became abuzz with interest in what facilities would be repaired first. The Vice President for Student Affairs even held a student town-hall meeting to best understand where students felt the greatest need was.

The dollar figure began to grow, and the Vice President for Administration was perhaps the busiest of any administrator on campus, revising the campus master plan and marking where temporary offices or classrooms might be constructed. A rough timeline was also being developed, with priorities being assigned so that student recruitment could be highlighted as new and renovated facilities came open.

President Havilland began to prepare her presentation to the Faculty Senate and Executive Council on how to pay for the campus renovation when she received her first setback. Dr. Jeff Clark, the longtime Vice President for Development met privately with the President and announced his intention to retire at the end of the year. Part of Clark's motivation might have been "breaking in" a new president, but there was possibly also some insight that his job was about to become much more difficult and challenging in raising money for all of the talked about new construction.

Clark's departure was even more unsettling to Havilland. She had been through transitions before, and knew that they could set development efforts back by years. She had a strong sense of Clark's network: he was well liked, he had a long history with virtually every major donor to the campus, he had a wonderful reputation for being ethical and putting donor needs and interests first, and most of all, he was an effective communicator who could bridge conflict. His skills had been invaluable, but his institutional historical knowledge would also be very much missed.

Havilland tried politely to convince Clark to stay, but he had made his decision. Havilland privately wondered if he was really as good as everyone had indicated, as the campus was not raising nearly as much money as she thought it should. Also, this would be an opportunity to put into place her own person. She made a quick phone call to her former colleague who worked in development, but he declined her interest in having him join her at JSU. She needed to get this position nailed down, or at least a strategy to fill the position, before she announced her plan.

Let's Pause Here

1. Is there anything President Havilland missed in working through her transition to the presidency? Might she have included major donors in her initial set of meetings, or is it more appropriate to wait until she started her new position to meet with these individuals.

2. If you were advising the President on how to set priorities, might you have done anything differently? Is moving fast always the smartest approach?

3. With Vice President Clark's retirement, what strategy would you recommend for President Havilland? Does it make any difference knowing that she came from a different institution and by some standards would be considered 'an outsider?'

4. In beginning to think about fundraising for facilities, what kind of motivational incentives can or should be considered? To what extent do you imagine naming opportunities of facilities a major incentive to give?

5. How important are facilities to your perceived philosophy of higher education? Are lazy rivers and private

apartment style residence hall rooms critical? Is this a fad in higher education, or is there an educational element to facilities that should be considered?

Havilland felt a growing pressure from herself, and she thought she also felt it from her board. She needed to keep her initial momentum up, and upon the recommendation of outgoing Vice President Clark, she appointed David Crone to the Vice President of Advancement position. Crone had spent the past five years as the Director of Development for the College of Business and seemed to be well respected by his peers. There were some in the office who thought Havilland should have promoted the Associate Vice President who had more experience, and they complained somewhat internally about Crone's lack of institutional wide experience.

With Crone's appointment finalized, Havilland publicly announced her plan, which included three major components, each of which must be successful if the plan is to be fully implemented. The plan did not rely on any state funds and, if successful, would enable the university to build new residence facilities and renovate existing academic buildings immediately.

The first part of the plan would be the implementation of a facility fee for all enrolled students. Two dollars per semester credit hour would be added to student fees each year for a total of $10 per semester credit hour in the fifth year of the plan. The impact on students would be $60 in the first year ($600,000 in student fee money in the first year) and $150 in the fifth year ($3 million).

JSU has been fortunate in that it has been able to keep tuition increases modest the last several years, and when compared with other state institutions, JSU is financially very competitive. The student government leadership was also very supportive of the plan to implement a facility fee for new and renovated facilities and voted unanimously to support President Havilland's plan.

The second component of the plan was to raise private funds that would be added to the revenue from the facility fee. JSU has been relatively successful in raising private funds from alumni, corporations, foundations and other friends of the University. Her appointment of Crone allowed her to highlight the success of the development program and use his new position to begin a new round of donor introductions and the creation of a new messaging campaign. JSU had completed a capital campaign four years ago and is already in the planning stages for another campaign in the not-too-distant future. While some donors are still paying on campaign pledges, donors and volunteers seem to be expecting another campaign and have already begun some preparations for another major effort.

The third component of the financing plan is to use tax exempt bonds for the construction projects. Most colleges and universities in the state have used tax-exempt bonds for construction projects so this is nothing new to the institution. The size of the bond issue will depend upon the amount of revenue collected from the facility fee and the amount that can be generated from private gifts. The hope is that it might be possible to divide the total project in thirds so that each component generates a third of the revenue required for the projects.

Various state and Federal laws permit certain types of debt financing for a variety of capital improvements, including buildings, on a tax exempt basis. The main advantage of this financing method is the lower interest cost in comparison to the interest rate on conventional debt available to a borrower.

Investors in tax exempt bonds do not have to pay

federal income tax on interest payments received on the bonds so these investors will accept an interest rate lower than the interest rate on comparable taxable bonds where the interest is subject to federal income taxation. Some states will exempt the interest on tax-exempt bonds from state income taxes which will make the bonds even more attractive to investors.

Havilland wrote up her plan in specific detail, providing specific dollar amounts to be raised from each element of her plan. She mailed over-night each board member a copy, cautious of freedom-of-information laws and wanting to keep her plan private for the moment. She then called each board member for their consent with the plan, and then planned a very public announcement of what her priority would be for the next several years.

Havilland publicly announced her plan by distributing it to her executive council (who had actually been intimately involved in its development), in a joint meeting of the faculty, student, and staff senates, and a public relations news release and web page dedicated to "Rebuilding Johnson!" The plans from the deans and vice presidents, prioritized, indicated that JSU would need just over $100 million in total revenue for the construction projects. Her new Vice President, Crone, planned a day of giving to capture the excitement and begin to build enthusiasm for the mini-campaign. He also developed a campaign strategy that included approaching some of JSU's larger donors, particularly those from the business sector with whom he had previous relationships.

Let's Pause Again

1. Do you note any major concerns with Havilland's plan? Do you perceive that finishing the current

capital campaign will negatively impact 'Rebuilding Johnson!,' and if so, how might that negativity be overcome?

2. What transitional steps should Vice President Crone be prepared to deal with? If you were to outline a transition plan for him, what steps would it include over a six month period of time?

3. Should any public officials be engaged in this discussion or this planning? How might raising private money and "taxing" students through a fee be perceived by state legislators?

4. Should Crone and Havilland tried the idea of raising money for facilities with any focus groups of potential donors? If so, what questions would you ask a focus group to assess their true interest in giving to a facilities campaign?

5. How would you measure the success of this plan? Should the focus be entirely on raising an adequate amount of money or are there other markers to assess its success? If so, what are they, and how are they measured? Can any of the plan be linked to student learning?

Initial fundraising is going quite well and constituents are responding to solicitations with generosity. Five year pledges are being secured and some sizable gifts are beginning to flow to the university. This has exuded confidence for the campaign committee, Havilland, and her new Vice President, Crone. The Board also approved the student facility fee, resulting in a collective feeling on campus that facilities were finally going to be brought up to a 'state of the art,' and the Admissions office adapted their recruitment materials to show what some of the renovated and new facilities would look like.

The development office, now under new leadership for the first time in 40 years, is using a standard pledge form for the campaign and the pledge form identifies the basic elements of the effort. These forms were printed in-house, meaning using the campus printing facilities, and Crone was pleased to see the low prices for printing these materials. Crone also had banners printed that he had hung on light-posts around campus that read "Rebuilding Johnson!" and a ceremonial first-shovel was held on the location of the residential hall expansion.

During a casual conversation between Crone and the Vice President for Administration and Finance, the subject of current pledges for the campaign was brought up. The Vice President for Administration and Finance was curious about the pledge activity for the reconstruction projects, and Crone offered to send over to her copies of the current pledges and campaign materials. Crone had a student worker get samples of all of the materials and walk them across campus to Administration and Finance that very afternoon.

Administration and Finance was not looking for any particular problem, but had simple curiosity about how Crone and his team were assembling such a successful development program so quickly. When the Vice President for Administration and Finance opened the campus mail envelope, she immediately felt there could be a problem. Upon inspection of the pledge forms, she realized that the way they were constructed could result in a problem for campus with arbitrage. The Vice President immediately telephoned the University's bond counsel and legal counsel.

"Thank you both for taking my call this afternoon," she opened the conference call. "I am not an expert on this, but I think I know enough to be dangerous. I think we have a problem with the way the pledge form is set up. What do you think?" she asked.

The bond counsel representative explained that federal tax statutes and regulations that govern the investment and expenditure of tax exempt bonds are quite definitive, and, that the differential between taxable and tax exempt interest rates can provide an opportunity for a philanthropic organization to recognize profits by borrowing at a low tax exempt rate and investing the proceeds at a higher taxable rate.

The bond representative continued, and the JSU legal counsel concurred, that this is not what Congress intended tax-exempt bonds to be used for, so Congress placed restrictions on controlling the amount of profit or "arbitrage" that can be realized by the borrower in tax exempt financing. Bond counsel explained that care must be exercised to avoid the characterization of bonds as "arbitrage bonds." The key to successful coordination of fundraising efforts and debt financing is to avoid the treatment of pledges and gifts as replacement proceeds of the bonds. Therefore the pledge form must be constructed in a way to refrain from tying it directly to the project. In other words the pledge form must be open ended and unrestricted so that the institution can use the funds pledged for other purposes. This way the gifts that are received from the pledges do not have to be applied to offset or repay financing for particular buildings.

Further, the bond counsel explained that pledges should not reference a particular building project where bonds are incurred and should be as unrestricted as possible. Probably the most effective way to structure the pledge form is to simply place responsibility for use of the gift in the hands of the governing board. Further investigation should be conducted to determine if current pledges using the pledge form should be refunded and re-issued by the donors.

Similarly, acknowledgement letters from the University should refrain from mentioning a specific capital project and be open ended in thanking the donor for their commitment. This will no doubt require an explanation to benefactors but bond counsel was insistent that this special language be used in all pledge forms.

The Vice President for Finance and Administration gathered her notes and did some additional research, requesting an immediate meeting with Crone, Havilland, and the other vice presidents. She laid out the conversation with the bond counsel, affirmed by the JSU legal counsel.

Havilland said, "I am not the least bit happy about his. David, weren't you aware of this?"

"Uh, no, not really," Crone stammered. "I just thought it was the most appropriate and honest way to proceed. I mean I've heard of arbitrage before, but…"

As Crone's comments drifted off, Havilland took control of the meeting. She began with charging Crone, and someone from legal counsel, to write a letter to all donors who had made a gift using the pledge form. She then charged Crone's office with fixing the pledge form, but having it approved by Finance and Administration and legal counsel as well. She also asked to get a preliminary legal decision based on the wording of the language. And lastly, she wanted a list of all $10,000 and higher donors who had used the pledge form and told Crone that he had to visit each of them personally and explain what had happened.

Havilland glared at Crone as he left the meeting, not knowing if this was a one-time, honest mistake by a new vice president, or if she had made a poor choice in the hiring for the sake of speed.

To Conclude the Discussion

1. Draft a letter for use by Crone and the development staff that will explain the error. Be sure to address the change in the gift, and be aware of the legal ramifications of what you might decide to write. Who should sign such a letter?
2. How was Crone to know about the IRS regulations? Should he have known enough to ask someone, or is the IRS regulation so vague and little-known that it was a simple mistake?
3. What should Havilland do with or to Crone? Was her desire to move quickly a sign of reckless behavior?
4. What might be the impact of this error on the overall Rebuilding Johsnon! campaign? How can unrestricted gifts be solicited for a campaign with such a name without violating arbitrage regulations?
5. How can development staff treat naming opportunities for new facilities if gifts must be classified as unrestricted? Is there a way to separate construction based on student fee money and issued bonds?

Case Study 10:
Demise of a College

Baxter College is a small liberal arts institution near the Great Lakes, with an undergraduate enrollment of 1,200 students. There are no graduate programs at Baxter, and the historical reputation of Baxter has been at the center of its identity. And although it is firmly and foremost a liberal arts college, several pre-professional programs had been added in recent years to try and appeal to more prospective students. The college's best recruiting, though, was the Legacy Program, calling upon former students to send their sons and daughters 'unto the halls of Baxter.'

Founded in 1842, Baxter is a well-respected academic institution, but has raised tuition significantly to help balance the budget. The realities of rising technology, health care, and labor costs have challenged the institution as no period of time in the past had. The college has taken fundraising somewhat seriously, but not overly so. The result is a small endowment of approximately $35 million, and despite the close-knit, family-like atmosphere of the college, there has been little culture and history of giving.

Recruiting mostly from the Great Lakes area, the college has relied on pockets of private high schools in Detroit, Chicago, Toledo, Cleveland, and Milwaukee to send their students to Baxter. In recent years, though, the college has struggled to produce an entering freshman class of 400 new students. Missing that enrollment target by even a few students can result in hundreds of thousands of dollars not flowing into the institution.

A confounding problem for Baxter are the high standards of the institution and its faculty. The collection of faculty is outstanding, hailing from Michigan, Penn State, Ohio State, Wisconsin, Northwestern, etc. All of the prominent universities of the mid-west have their degree recipients teaching at Baxter. Baxter, in turn, has not compromised its admissions standards or classroom standards, and the result is that it is not uncommon to lose 75 students between the first semester and the second. At a tuition rate of $45,000 per year, that is a loss of over $3.3 million in tuition revenue per year!

Members of the Board of Trustee have been curious about the work of the faculty for some time. A common discussion relates to whether faculty have unreal expectations for Baxter students, and whether or not the faculty truly have the best interests of the students at heart, or if they seem to enjoy running students off to other institutions. This, Board members say, keeps class sizes small and the arrogance level of faculty high.

Baxter's enrollment and retention issues are not unique, as they are similar to many small, private liberal arts colleges that have a history in individual philanthropy, but have struggled to keep pace with changes throughout the higher education landscape. Baxter's administration had attempted an online graduate degree to raise cash and expand the 'brand' of Baxter, but faculty push back ultimately led to it being closed down after only two years. The administration had attempted to revamp the online program to raise cash, using adjunct faculty and several high profile business leaders as 'guest speakers' or 'guest instructors,' and this had helped some, but not significantly.

In an effort to find additional cash, the administration had begun spending from the college's restricted endowment. Initially, the college viewed this as an emergency, short-term strategy to prevent faculty lay-offs, but the practice continued without too much long-term thinking. Without a plan in place to resolve enrollment and retention issues, the college's administration continued spending on the endowment for 30 consecutive years without a negative consequence. The practice went largely unnoticed until a certified letter landed on the President's desk.

Stacy May, the President's secretary, signed for the certified letter and cautiously opened the large envelope from the State Attorney General's office. A similar letter was delivered to Cole Statford, the Chairman of the Board of Trustees. The letter was an official notice and request for records on the spending patterns of Baxter College regarding endowment income and whether the college had inappropriately spent restricted donor contributions. The case specifically claimed or challenged that gifts that were designated for certain activities, such as scholarship funds, were being used to subsidize the operation of the institution in other ways, such as covering payroll.

In a closed Board session, Stratford led a vote to fire and replace the President. The President had been at the helm of the college for 13 years and was popular among the faculty and students, but the Board members, to a person, believed that he had not been effective in managing the finances of the college or raising the money or garnering the enrollment necessary to make the institution financially stable. This vote was not a huge surprise, as the finances of the college had been unstable for the past decade. The inquiry by the State Attorney General's office was a 'nail in the coffin,' as one Board member put it.

An added concern voiced by the Board as they met in private was what they believed to be the poor performance of the development office. Only 8% of the alumni body was making a gift to the college, and the Vice President for Advancement position had been open for the past three months. Prior to the latest opening in the position, five people had held the job in four years. Board members did not know if this was a function of poor presidential leadership or if there was some systemic problem with the office. Change was desperately needed if the college was to stay open.

The last piece of evidence the Board had discussed was a wealth management screening; a list of names with giving potential that had been contracted to an outside vendor for the institution. The screening confirmed what the Board had believed, that there was a high capacity for giving, but that these individuals had not been cultivated or asked to support the institution.

Let's Pause Here

1. If you are on the Board of Trustees, what are your priorities for the short- and long-term? What challenge do you take on first? Why and what are the consequences of this prioritization?
2. What should the College's response be to the Attorney General's inquiry? Is there a benefit to taking one stance rather than another? How public should the College be in drafting their response?
3. Do the faculty have any blame to accept for the financial status of the College? What concerns would you have about retention and increasing graduation rates?
4. Is there a place in the higher education industry for a college like Baxter? What role or niche does it fill,

and what characteristics of students can or should be the target audience of such a college?

5. What is your thinking about the state of fundraising at Baxter? Recognizing that there has been little cultivation and stewardship activity, where would you recommend starting to place your efforts in the short-term?

The Board, conscious of costs, conducted their own search for a new president. Not having conducted a search in sometime, the process moved much slower than anyone anticipated, and after nearly a full year, a new president was hired. Dr. Emily Procter was hired from the Pittsburgh, Pennsylvania area where she was serving as the president of an online university. The Board was impressed with her ability raise cash from online programs and her strong business sense. If not an academic leader, she most certainly understood budgets and creating priorities.

Procter was briefed thoroughly by the Board and by the senior administrative team before her arrival, and on her first day, she issued an administrative mandate that all hiring and vacant positions would be frozen until she could work through a budget revision. By "freezing" the budget, she meant that no position would be filled unless she, herself, granted permission.

The Faculty Council, Baxter's version of a 'faculty senate' and sometimes referred to as "The Apostles," issued a letter to Proctor asking for full budget disclosure and demanding to know by which criteria she, the newcomer, would decide which positions would be filled. Procter learned that the name "Apostles" was given to the leadership of the Council because they felt that they were really in charge of the College and wielded a significant amount of power over the actions of the College.

Procter believed in shared governance, but felt that there was a time and place for more direct action. She sent a conciliatory email to the Council indicating that she would meet with them "in due time." The Council leadership had not been communicated with in such a fashion under the previous administration and immediately started secret meetings talking about how to approach the new president. The 'water cooler' conversation seemed to indicate that "this new president won't last a year!"

The majority of Procter's work during her first weeks was focused on the budget, revenue, and expenditures. She discovered that the college has actually been spending restricted endowment funds to cover deficit spending, an action that was clearly inappropriate and perhaps even illegal. She contracted with a private attorney in Detroit to respond to the Attorney General's letter, which the Board had gotten a continuance on. The attorney, who was not inexpensive, bargained with the Attorney General's office to put in place a new management plan for the Baxter endowment and to pay a fine.

As the Attorney General response was being concluded, Procter finally had a clear financial picture of where the College stood and what kind of financial future it might or could have. Canceling the Baxter Board holiday party, she called an emergency meeting of the Executive Committee. The day-long meeting was held at the Cadillac Hotel, and Procter felt a certain appropriateness in having such a serious discussion in a hotel that had been built by Detroit's struggling auto industry. The agenda had one item: Baxter College Financial Situation.

Procter's senior administration sat with her as she delivered a comprehensive analysis of the financial situation of the institution. The College was losing money every month and had, as they all now knew, been illegally spending restricted endowment income. Based on the financial projections of Procter and the College's administration, the College was in serious jeopardy of closing at the end of the year. She itemized the College's assets and also indicated that if they could sell the college property at market value, the Board would be able to pay almost all of the College's current debts and would not be responsible for any further obligations. Further, Procter walked through a process of closing a college in accordance with AAUP guidelines, including timelines for notifying students and faculty of the cancelation of their contracts.

The Board members were incredulous with this news and indicated that they felt they had not been kept fully informed by the previous president. The Board of Trustees formed a special committee to review the College's finances and confirm the new president's findings. Procter communicated bluntly with the Board that such confirmation work was appropriate, and responsible, but that it needed to be handled quickly. She further informed the Board that she intended to hire a temporary Vice President for Development, someone to help raise much needed capital. She worked with a fundraising consulting firm and hired a consultant on an 18-month contract.

As the Board set about their exploratory work, with a spring meeting deadline, Procter and her new Vice President for Development decided that it was their responsibility to inform the alumni body of Baxter of the serious nature of the College's financial situation. They knew that this could spread panic among the alumni body, and cause mass resignations among the faculty. And despite a very frank presentation to the Faculty Council, many faculty members believed that Procter was "overreacting" and that her prior experience precluded her from understanding the deep-intellectualism among the Baxter family.

By February 1, the Faculty Council had drafted a no-confidence vote resolution to the Board about President Procter. The Provost announced his resignation to accept a similar position at a different college in the West. Some faculty began looking for other jobs, and although there had been no public announcement of the College's financial situation, fall enrollment projections were even lower than previous years.

Let's Pause Again

1. What should be Procter's approach to working with the Faculty Council? Should she consider them a strong constituency that needs to be placated, or are they being obstructionist and part of the problem?
2. Will announcing the financial state of the college cause panic among alumni? How might they craft an effective message to raise money and educate the alumni body without creating fear about the future of the college?
3. Should the Board be doing something different in response to the crisis? What role should they be playing in establishing a more firm and stable financial base for the College?
4. The use of a "temporary" administrator is not unusual in higher education, and many professional associations often work with retired or retiring administrators to create 'administrators-on-loan' programs. Is this an advisable strategy for Baxter College? Does hiring a "temporary" development officer raise concerns about the future of the College? What messaging would you use to introduce this new employee to the campus and alumni constituency?
5. What other considerations should Procter be consider-

ing? Should she be looking at alternative ways to close the college, such as merging with other liberal arts colleges? Should she be considering closing different academic departments to keep others open?

The Vice President for Development wrote a letter that would be sent to all alumni informing them of the severity of the crisis. Additionally, he created a website called "The Future of Baxter" that contained the letter. The letter, and the website, asked alumni to respond generously with their gifts before the end of the fiscal year, pulled no punches, and was very definitive about a looming fiscal crisis. The letter and website indicated that Baxter needed $10 million to cover essential payroll for the remainder of the fiscal year, and the projected deficit for the next fiscal year was about the same, just over $10 million. The letter closed by asking alumni and friends of the College "to search your heart, remembering the time you spent on the Baxter campus, and to give future generations that same opportunity."

A slightly modified copy of the letter was also sent to a targeted list of 3,000 alumni who had been screened as having the ability to make a six figure gift. These letters also indicated that several meetings of alumni in key area cities were going to be held to talk about how they could help save Baxter.

The website included a video message from both the President and Stratford as Chairman of the Board. RSVP links were embedded with information on the alumni meetings, and stressed throughout all of the communications was the need for immediate support to keep the college open.

The first meeting was held at another historic hotel, the Scoffield, in downtown Cleveland. The stately old hotel provided a meeting room with seating for 200, and Procter was disappointed when she took the podium with a less than half-filled room. She began her remarks celebrating the history and founding of the college, showing photographs throughout her presentation about the founding of the college, the first buildings and graduates, and through visual images of buildings, began to show deterioration and the problems with capital upkeep. She showed pictures of three faculty members sharing an office, of wiring that was not contained in hallways, and even a picture of a student pushing an a/v cart across campus in the snow. She moved onto the financial portion of her presentation, highlighting faculty salaries, the increasing costs of technology, and in an image that was marred in red-ink, an overall budget snapshot that showed Baxter's $10 million shortfall for the current fiscal year. Her last image was of the college's Old Main building with a real estate sign photo-shopped in front of it, meaning that the college would close if money was not raised immediately.

She let the last image rest on the screen and sink in with the audience members, and then asked them if they had questions, ideas for raising needed resources, or just wanted to talk about the state of the college.

An elderly gentleman rose and walked to the microphone. "Back at the beginning of your talk, that was Adele, my wife and me, in the picture of the kids having a picnic on the blanket," he said. "This school really means a lot to me, and Madame President, you have my full support."

Several other alumni followed with similar comments of adoration for the college and promises of financial support. The comments stirred President Procter as she began to feel confident that alumni support would flow in. Then a middle-aged man strode to the microphone.

"Well, I guess I appreciate your coming down here

to talk to us," he began. "But I've got a question for you. How much do you make?"

Procter was a bit taken aback by the direct nature of his comments and began to respond when he stopped her mid-sentence and began a tirade.

"I've read all about what's going on in higher education today. Six figure salaries, expensive golden parachutes, big screen tv sets in the dorm, and all the while, you sit in your ivory tower and let kids get drunk while charging them ridiculous tuition! And, I hear that girls are getting raped every day on campus, and you are coming down here asking us for money!"

Procter sternly looked at the speaker and asked what year he graduated in. Without responding, he dropped the microphone, muttering, "you're all the same" and walked out. Procter recovered the meeting as best she could, giving instructions for the staff who were around the room to work with individuals on pledge cards and to arrange individual meetings.

Meetings of alumni in six other cities followed the same pattern of generally supportive comments with a few negative statements or questions sprinkled through the commentary. After two months of aggressive meetings and public pleas, the college had raised $5.5 million. Little had come in from the mailings, as the website had been more productive. The mid-western cities tour had been more successful, and despite the love for the institution and the seemingly endless stream of emails that flooded Procter's inbox, it became apparent to her that there was no way they would be able to make their $10 million goal.

The language in the letter, in her presentations, and on the website had been clear: without a minimum of $10 million, they would not be able to meet their payroll obligations for the current fiscal year. The AAUP file on her desk that contained dozens of pages about protocol for fiscal distress had become dog-eared. The stack of credit card receipts for which she was owed reimbursement for her travels sat on her desk in a different file, and she quietly wondered if she could even get reimbursed.

Procter had an appointment scheduled with her Vice President for Development in an hour, but she knew in her heart what the future for Baxter was, and she picked up the telephone to call the Chairman of the Board.

To Conclude the Discussion

1. To what extent did the Board of Trustees bear ultimate responsibility for not realizing the financial condition of the college? If they did not have knowledge of the financial situation, should they have?
2. Should criminal charges be filed for spending restricted endowment? Write a general letter to the alumni of the college explaining the spending of restricted endowment gifts.
3. Is it advisable to appeal to alumni for what is essentially debt reduction? What would be the motivations, risks, and benefits of appealing to alumni for such an activity - will alumni be generous if they believe the college is in jeopardy of closing?
4. Procter's relationship to the faculty appeared to be contentious. What message should she be sending to them, how might she use them as an advocate, and ultimately, what approach should faculty be taking with the extreme fiscal situation of the college?
5. If Procter decides, and Stratford and the Board agree, to close the college, what can you identify as the impact on pledged gifts, past donors, and those who have given to the college for endowments, such as

scholarships? What is the responsible messaging that should come from the President and Board?

Case Study 11:
Protection of Donor Information

Delta Southwestern University is a prominent public institution of approximately 17,000 students. The student body is composed primarily of students from the southeastern United States but sees as a point of pride that it has a student from every state in the country. The majority of the enrollment, however, is from its home and bordering states along the Mississippi River.

The average DSU test score is a 23 on the ACT exam, because of its relatively low-cost and proximity in the south, it has a number of first-generation students as well as minority students, primarily African Americans and Hispanics. These students tend to be from less-affluent families with limited resources, which makes student financial aid and private scholarship support extremely important.

The President of the University is Dr. Paschal "Paulie" Smith, who has enjoyed much success at the institution where he has served in the role for 12 years. His success in fundraising is legendary and he is highly respected by students, faculty and alumni. The Board of Trustees of DSU recently gave him a new five-year contract which recognized his considerable leadership talent.

The Vice President for Development, Karen Sergeant, is also well respected by the university's constituents and has been with the institution for six years having come from a major public research university in Michigan. The President and Vice President have made a good team in development and have increased annual giving by over 50% in the last five years. Most of the funds raised have supported the renovation of old facilities and an investment in Delta Regional Studies. The campus leadership believes it is now time to turn attention to building the endowment.

The DSU endowment is about $80 million, considered low for an institution of its size and scope. The university is launching a major capital campaign to enhance the endowment, hoping to raise funds for endowed professorships, chairs and student scholarships for first-generation students. President Smith has indicated that student scholarships are the highest priority in the capital campaign and wants to raise several million dollars to benefit poor students.

One of the university's major benefactors is the founder and owner of a large coal company with several mining facilities throughout the United States. The country's political climate has swung back to mining coal aggressively and the Amalgamated Coal Company (ACC) is having a banner year in financial growth. Although there was an environmental student group who opposed ACC's work in strip mining, most of the campus and community are silent on the involvement of the coal company as a donor to the university.

The head of the company and primary owner is Thaddeus Thompson who graduated from the University in 1948. He is a first generation student who came to the University on a full scholarship immediately after World War II. Mr. Thompson benefited from the G.I. Bill and knows the importance of scholarship support first hand, as it allowed him to obtain a degree in geological sciences and go on to form an international company respected around the world.

Amalgamated Coal has become one of the largest coal producers in the United States, focusing on under-mined areas of the mid-west and upper southeast. Although ACC is a public company, Thompson owns the majority of the stock and it is estimated that he is worth well over $500 million. Mr. Thompson is 90 years old but in reasonable health for a man of his age, and has indicated to President Smith that he wants to do something "major" for the institution. Recognizing the great importance of scholarship support in his own life, Thompson has decided to create a sizable endowment at DSU primarily for first-generation students who have financial need.

Recently, President Smith and Vice President for Development Sergeant, who have been cultivating Mr. Thompson for several years, met with him and discussed his interest in a major gift to the university. They were hoping that they might develop and place a proposal before Mr. Thompson for $25 million, which would be the largest gift in the history of the University. Much to their shock and pleasant surprise Mr. Thompson indicated to them that he was thinking of a much larger gift of $100 million for scholarships for needy students.

However, Mr. Thompson made it clear that he wanted to be certain that such a gift would make a measurable impact on both the University and the entire state. "I want to help transform this part of the country," he told Smith and Sergeant. "I've spent my whole life living right around here, and yes, I've got some resources now, and I want to help everybody. And, I think through you two and Delta, I can."

Thompson's country-boy image and slow, casual

cadence of speech masked the fact that he is a methodical decision-maker and is known to research any major decision he makes by using a number of expert consultants. Mr. Thompson made it clear to Smith and Sergeant that he would not make the gift unless he was absolutely convinced of its potential impact on the university and the state.

As Smith and Sergeant climbed into their car to drive back to campus, Sergeant looked over at Smith with a huge grin, commenting "$100 million! Can you believe that old guy! This is going to be huge!"

Smith responded, "We don't have it yet. Far from it. We need to figure out how his gift will impact the state, and we have to prove it to him. And with hard numbers."

Let's Pause Here

1. Is it appropriate for a president to have such a strong agenda for creating a capital campaign? Although President Smith has an altruistic goal of first-generation student scholarship support, should a feasibility study identify where they can raise money, or should the priority be set and then the goal be established?
2. Should Smith and Sergeant have been surprised that Thompson was thinking about $100 million when they targeted him at $25 million? Is this a reflection of a lack of preparation?
3. In the cultivation of Thompson, the DSU leaders hoped to place a proposal in front of him, meaning ask him for a gift. Should they have had that outlined with specific talking points prior to this meeting? If so, draft four or five key talking points that they could use to communicate their interests to Thompson.
4. What do you make of Thompson's desire to see his

gift impact "the state" and not just the university? Is this a responsibility for the DSU administration? How would you approach demonstrating such an impact?
5. What are the next steps, and timeline, for Smith and Sergeant?

President Smith checked with several of his peer presidents at other institutions, and ultimately decided to spend about $25,000 to hire a major New York consulting company to provide data on the impact such a gift would make on the university and state. He decided to use his unrestricted gift account to pay for the consultant so that he would not have to go through the university's public contract bidding process.

The president wanted to show that the investment of $100 million in scholarships for students would not only benefit hundreds of students far into the future, but also would be an economic development provider for the entire state. By educating the sons and daughters of the local working class, President Smith hoped to show that the students would stay in the state and help benefit the economy. He believed personally that this would resonate with Mr. Thompson and show him that his $100 million gift would be a massive economic incentive to the state. He began to use the word "transformational" when discussing the possible $100 million gift.

Smith asked Sergeant to lead the work with the consultant and spend whatever time and additional resources were necessary to produce the important research that would convince Thompson that his gift would truly make a difference. Vice president Sergeant was also tasked with the responsibility of coordinating with the consulting firm in creating a proposal that they could place before Thompson.

Because of Thompson's advanced age, they felt that timing was "of the essence" and that they needed to move judiciously and with haste on developing the proposal and delivering it to Thompson. In an update to Thompson, Sergeant told him "we've been working night and day to really do a deep study of the impact of your potential gift, and I think we can have some result and a proposal to you in the next two months." Thompson seemed very pleased.

Davidson Consulting Company of Manhattan, New York has helped numerous philanthropic clients with high-level research similar to what is being requested by DSU. The consulting firm has teamed up with numerous foundations, corporations and individuals in providing support and consultation services on philanthropic matters. They are a well-regarded firm nationally and have access to materials and information that have been very helpful to a number of philanthropists nation-wide. They even had a division specifically targeted at higher education clients, like DSU.

After numerous phone calls and meetings with the consulting firm, a proposal was created that made a strong case for the $100 million investment by Thompson. The proposal was over 150 pages long and contained a large amount of research on the impact such a gift would have on economic development, including additions to the tax base, the education of the labor force, and even quality of life indicators. President Smith was ultimately very pleased with the proposal generated and decided he was ready to place it before Thompson.

On December 10 President Smith and Vice President Sergeant went to Thompson's home and over coffee at his kitchen table, delivered the proposal to him. The ask amount was for $100 million, as Thompson had indicated, and the President and Vice President spent two hours with Thompson going over every detail of the proposal.

Thompson, well known for his poker face, said very little and indicated to the two gentlemen that he wanted to study the proposal further before making any final decisions. Thompson indicated that he would probably hire a second consulting firm to advise him on the proposal. President Smith was a little concerned about the need for another consulting firm but felt he should not mention his concern to Thompson as it might have a negative impact on the proposal. Thompson asked the President to give him another 30 days before he made a decision, and the meeting concluded with a warm and hearty handshake.

Both Smith and Sergeant left the meeting somewhat perplexed as they really thought the proposal would be accepted immediately and started to feel as though Thompson might possibly back out of the verbal commitment. There was not much they could do but to wait for Thompson to hire his consultant, review the proposal, and be patient. Obviously, with the stakes being so high they left the meeting quite nervous and concerned, but committed to moving forward. As the two walked from their parking space in front of their office building, Old Main, Smith turned to Sergeant and said, "Well, let's get that major donor prospect list back out and start looking at our next line of gifts. Come up around 4:30 this afternoon and we'll get started."

Two weeks went by with no word from Thompson, and Sergeant made a courtesy phone call, just to 'check in.' Thompson indicated that he had indeed hired a consulting firm, Community Development Consulting (CDC) out of Boston, and that they would be in touch. Less than a week later, the project consultant from CDC phoned Sergeant and began asking questions about the university. Questions then turned to community economic development, endowment management strategy, and even the enrollment management plan of DSU. Sergeant was confused after the hour and half phone call, but that confusion turned to concern when the same project consultant called back every day during the next week with a broad range of questions that spanned faculty credentials to President Smith's personal health.

Both Smith and Sergeant could feel the gift slipping away and were extremely concerned that the new consulting firm would kill the proposal. Sergeant began doing research on CDC, but found nothing that would lead him to believe that there was a hidden agenda in their past work. Smith's enthusiasm for the entire campaign began to waiver, and he privately wondered if putting so much hope into Thompson had been an error in judgement.

A few days later, Thompson called President Smith and asked him a question that was most troubling. Thompson wanted Smith to explain to him why it would not be better for him to invest his money in bringing in startup companies as well as new high end corporations to the community for economic development purposes. Thompson said that $100 million placed strategically could be a huge incentive for a number of companies to locate in the region thereby spawning new jobs. "Wouldn't this have a better impact on the community then the scholarship proposal?" Thompson asked.

Smith felt sure that Thompson's consulting company had put this idea in his mind and was not sure how to strategically move the discussion back to their scholarship proposal.

Smith explained how $100 million investment would help to keep some of the brightest students in the region thereby contributing to the state's economy. He talked about the brain drain that had plagued the University and state for years and that what the region really needed was intellectual human capital. Thompson understood the importance of scholarships but wondered if these students who he helped would have jobs when they graduated from college. At this point in the conversation, Smith became extremely concerned and visibly shaken, and could see the $100 million dollar gift moving to a different priority.

Let's Pause Again

1. Do you think that Thompson hired his own company to "fact-check" that of DSU's consulting company, or did he simply want his own, independent opinion? Should the DSU administration have been surprised that he hired his own company?

2. Smith and Sergeant obviously want the $100 million gift from Thompson. What should their strategy be at this time? To what extent do they make a hard push for the gift, and to what extent do they sit back and let Thompson make his own decision?

3. What other institutional information might Smith and Sergeant put in front of Thompson to help him guide the gift in their direction?

4. How might Smith and Sergeant engage students to help influence Thompson in making his decision? Be specific and make a recommendation on how they might be used, in what ways, and when?

5. Without Thompson's gift, the idea of the capital campaign is in jeopardy of not meeting its fundraising goal. What course of action should Sergeant be taking right now in the event that the Thompson gift does not materialize?

After a month of hearing nothing from Thompson, Smith invited him to a dinner at the president's home, purely as a stewardship event, expressing gratitude for all Thompson has done for DSU. In addition to Smith, the dinner included 'the usual suspects' of staff members and university leaders.

Thompson arrived on time in his chauffeur driven car. He was in good spirits and enjoyed several drinks with the staff, whom he saw as friends, before sitting down to dinner. Toward the end of the evening Thompson suddenly blurted out, "well Mr. President, I haven't heard from you in quite a while and was wondering where our proposal stood."

Smith was certain that the next step was for Thompson to contact him, but he did not show his frustration, and responded, "Well, I didn't really want to bring that up tonight. But, we can talk about it anytime you might want to."

"I want to right now," Thompson responded quickly. A hush fell over the dinner table as he continued. "I've been thinking about this, a lot, and I've decided to go ahead with the $100 million gift. Half for scholarships for first generation students, and the other for those high achieving, really smart kids."

As the largest gift in the university's history, Sergeant's staff moved quickly to finalize the gift and make a public announcement. They coordinated with Thompson for a major press conference in the lobby of the DSU Old Main building, and distributed the press releases and accompany photographs to the staff hours before the press conference began.

The announcement of the gift was well received, as the local press outlets were thrilled to report on the gift and what it meant for the students and future of DSU.

One local paper, *The Daily River*, however, issued an op-ed piece about donor influence in university decision making. The author of the editorial wondered what kind of influence Thompson was getting in return for his gift, if he was typically "wined and dined" at the president's home, if he was going to the football games for free, and if with this substantial gift, he was "controlling the future student body of our public institution."

Sergeant's staff was in full swing with the Thompson gift and the capital campaign, and despite much state-wide positive media, *The River* kept hounding DSU about the Thompson gift. As Sergeant's staff, and President Smith, answered many of their questions, they finally threw up their hands at the realization that the paper was not going to report anything positive.

The editor of *The River* felt the frustration of DSU not disclosing the information on the gift, and filed a Freedom of Information Act (FOIA) request for the gift proposal and supporting documentation concerning the Thompson gift.

Smith's office had a strategy for handling these FOIA requests, and he immediately handed it off to the appropriate person in Sergeant's office. The internal machine went to work and produced over 300 pages of email messages and internal documents about the Thompson gift, going back almost five years. Some of the messages were slightly embarrassing, as the tone of some of the email messages were very casual. None, though were particularly damaging.

The staff at *The River* went to work digging through the materials, and within two days threatened to file a lawsuit against DSU if they did not disclose the entire gift proposal, including the 150 page consultant report.

Sergeant's staff worked through the University Legal

Counsel to issue a statement that the consultant's report was proprietary information and could not and should not be included with the other information. *The River* threatened to sue DSU for the entire report, including the costs associated with having the report conducted.

DSU released the receipt for having the report conducted, and *The River* was happy to report that the university was not complying with the state disclosure FOIA law and that they must be hiding something.

The newspaper immediately filed a law suit in state court demanding that DSU release the entire report. Sergeant personally called the editor of the newspaper explaining that report was proprietary in nature and contained a great deal of personal information concerning the donor. The editor reminded Sergeant that just about anything should be released that is considered to be a public record, with few exceptions. A public record is defined as any writing, sound or video that reflects the performance or lack of performance of an official function. All records maintained by public employees within the scope of their employment are presumed to be public records.

One of the few exemptions to what types of records are available under the law are files that if disclosed would give advantage to competitors. Sergeant's thinking was that releasing the consultant's report would give other organizations an advantage over the University and allow them to see how the University went about soliciting one of their largest prospects. *The River's* position was that there must be something in the proposal that the university and Thompson did not want released, surmising that the university had given something to Thompson or his company in return for the $100 million gift. The newspaper publisher told Smith that it looks as though Thompson is buying the University with his gift. The newspaper simply could not understand that anyone would make a $100 million gift without getting something in return. They suspected that the quid pro quo was revealed in the proposal and they absolutely demanded to see the proposal.

After consultation with the Chairman of the Board of Trustees, Smith decided to stand his ground and refuse the release of the document. As the lawsuit went forward, the refusal to disclose the 150 page proposal appeared in the daily headlines repeatedly, and guest editorials began to appear all questioning the integrity of Smith and the DSU leadership.

As Smith, Sergeant, and the Chairman of the Board, climbed the steps of the courthouse with the legal counsel, the senior attorney placed his hand on Smith's shoulder and told him, "This could really go either way, but to be honest, I'm not optimistic. Are you sure you don't want to try and cut some sort of deal?

To Conclude the Discussion

1. With the gift of $100 million being a surprise, is there anything that Smith and Sergeant should or could have done differently to anticipate the response they got from Thompson? Did they risk 'leaving money on the table' by not asking for enough?

2. What is the real risk to Smith and DSU if the document must be disclosed to the newspaper? What should the University be doing in advance of that ruling?

3. How should Smith and Sergeant be communicating with Thompson? What should be the central talking points they keep in front of him?

4. Was rushing to announce the gift the correct thing to do? Should the DSU administration have anticipated the FOIA request and perhaps release a somewhat

redacted copy of the report? Should they have anticipated such a request, and gotten an opinion from the State Attorney General in advance?

5. What should DSU's position be if they win the case and do not have to release the report? Would you anticipate that the newspaper will continue to be difficult on what they see as the 'secrecy' of the gift? What strategy might they come up with in advance to develop a better working relationship with *The River*?

Case Study 12:
Philanthropy Intersects with Eminent Domain

Cane Ridge University is a state public institution of approximately 12,000 students, and it is a relatively young institution, founded in 1965. CRU had its beginnings as a senior university, offering only the junior and senior year of a four-year degree, but in the past 20 years has expanded to offering all four-years of a bachelor's degree along with several professional master's degrees.

Cane Ridge was founded by a controversial governor who was very much loved during his tenure in the Governor's Mansion. There had been a rumor when CRU was founded that he had wanted it to be a "Black" school, part of his segregationist ideas that were popular at the time. There was also a rumor that he wanted to create the university so that his brother-in-law could be a college president. Regardless, as a political pet project, it was specifically developed to educate this southeastern state's youth of moderate academic ability. Cane Ridge never had a goal of trying to compete with the other big universities in the state for the most talented students, and often couched its recruiting materials around the idea of 'opportunity.'

As an institution for first-generation college students, CRU had a strong relationship with the legislature, partially because it was successful at enrolling a very diverse student population. Nearly 40% of the students at CRU

---

are African American, 40% are White, and nearly 20% are now Hispanic. Such diversity has been seen as an institutional strength and proof that a public higher education institution in the Deep South could be diverse.

The President of Cane Ridge is Dr. Trevor X. Cogdell who came from a prominent university in Georgia where he had served as provost. Dr. Cogdell, an African-American and economist by training, was well qualified to take over the university. After eight years as president, he finally came up with a plan to increase revenue and improve the overall campus. He had stabilized enrollment, but understood that he needed cash to improve both the facilities and faculty salaries, neither of which were bad, but both needed some improvement. His plan was to increase student enrollment to closer to 20,000, something most thought to be impossible.

As part of the enrollment growth plan, Cogdell anticipated that the freshmen class would live on campus, and perhaps even sophomores, but that meant that the composition of the freshmen class must change, and CRU must be seen as a 'destination' campus. This means that residence hall space must grow from its 1,800 beds to something closer to 5,000. The staff in the Division of Student Affairs were thrilled with this news, and began dreaming of living and learning communities, in-residence hall recreation centers, and even expand the recreation center.

Cogdell saw the expansion of enrollment by 8,000 students to reflect a change for the university. No longer would Cane Ridge be a school of 'opportunity' or 'first-chances,' but a destination that could compete with the best public universities in the state. He envisioned greater competition for admission, and he knew that in order to transform the university, he would have to be very aware of how the campus looked and 'felt.' He wanted to make the 1965 architecture look old and historic; he wanted to build a campus that would be more traditional.

Not everyone, though, was pleased with Cogdell's plan for enrollment increases. A group of local citizens, calling themselves "Keep Town and Gown Equal" were vocal about the issue and did not believe that city planners could accommodate such a large influx of students. Their Facebook page became popular very quickly, and many citizens highlighted projected problems with city services such as fire and police protection, basic infrastructure for healthcare, traffic, parking, etc. Several historic neighborhoods near campus had already complained to Cogdell about student parking on their narrow streets, and the mayor and two city council members similarly began communicating with Cogdell about his growth plans.

These community citizens also had concerns about the Greek life system on the CRU campus, often referring to them as "Animal House in the South." The reality of the Greek system was that these students had among the highest retention rates, highest post-graduation giving rates, and among the best grade point averages on campus. Cogdell saw them as simply being less refined than Greek participating students on other campuses. Cogdell did note, though, that the fraternities and sororities were very segregated, but also noted little friction between the groups.

Cogdell was little bit surprised when the Vice President for Student Affairs, Sally Adams, came into his office with news that one of the fraternities wanted to build a new house, completely with alumni money, and increase their bed space from 32 to 100. Cogdell had not anticipated new bed space in the Greek system, at least not very seriously, and was quite intrigued by the idea.

Beta Theta Nu, a national fraternity, had a solid reputation on campus and at first glance, neither Cogdell nor Adams had a problem with the idea. Cogdell began to think that if each of the 12 houses on campus re-built, there would be an opportunity to create a 'Greek-Row" type of environment and it would also reduce the commitment of the university to build so much more resident hall space.

The Beta chapter had a few difficulties with racially charged situations in the past decade, but nothing since Cogdell's first year on campus. He charged Adams with setting up a meeting with the campus planners and the senior university leadership to talk through the possible building. He also wanted to make sure that the development staff was in the meeting, as there would have to be a decision about using university property, raising money for the house, sanctioning it for first or second year students, etc.

The meeting reveals that the Beta alumni and their national chapter can afford a nearly $6 million fraternity house, but that they want the university to contribute the land. They also want the university to grant approval for first and second year students to be able to live in the house and they suggested housing and meal costs information to give the university a sense of what students might be expected to pay.

Let's Pause Here

1. To what extent does Cogdell's plans represent mission creep? Should he have to convince anyone at the state level that the university's mission and direction be changed, or does he have the authenticity to make this change by himself?
2. What are the benefits and disadvantages of becoming a 'destination' campus? What might the academic consequences be for the existing faculty and staff?

3. Should Cogdell have met with civic leaders prior to announcing his decision to try and increase enrollment? Should he have consulted early on about increasing enrollment?
4. Do you see any risks associated with enhancing the Greek-life environment on campus? Is it the best idea to take the fraternity that comes first to build a new house, or should there be some sort of equitable offer to any fraternity?
5. What are the financial risks and benefits to changing the university's policy to allow freshmen and sophomores to live in a fraternity or sorority house? Considering that Greek-chapter alumni are the most loyal supporters to the university, should any special considerations be given to them?

The senior leadership team of the university all agreed that the fastest way to begin expanding enrollment and changing the look and feel of campus would be to not only allow, but help Beta Theta Nu build a new house. The fraternity wants to build on a piece of property that is currently an eyesore for the university, an old auto body shop directly across from the campus. Even the community likes the idea of 'cleaning up the block' by removing the old auto body shop.

As the university does not own the auto body shop, and the Board of Trustees will need to condemn the property under eminent domain, Cogdell has asked the Board to begin proceedings. Eminent domain is the power of the government to take private property belonging to citizens for public use, provided just compensation is paid to the owner. The process can also be called "condemnation," or in some states, "expropriation." The basic concept is that the wishes of the people for the public good take precedent over the wishes of one, in this case, the auto body shop owner.

No one anticipates any problems in condemning the property and paying a fair price to the auto body shop so that the fraternity can proceed with its building project. The university would own the real estate and lease it to the fraternity on a long-term lease provision. The fraternity would build the new house at no cost to the institution through philanthropy from its alumni.

Nearly a decade ago, the fraternity had gotten in trouble for some racial issues. Some members, at that time, had taken to sitting on the front porch of their small house and would yell racial-epitaphs at those passing by. They also became embroiled in a membership dispute when they apparently refused to accept a Muslim student as a member. At the time, before Adams had joined the university, the fraternity had been suspended. Even though this was a long time ago, there were still some feelings among different populations that the Beta's were a 'racist' group.

One of the members of the Board of Trustees is a wealthy African American entrepreneur who has a number of apartment complexes in the city. Trustee Darius Jackson has been on the board for 8 years and is scheduled to become the Board Chairman in the last year of his 10 year term. He has been controversial, especially speaking out on issues of racial equity. He is an alumnus of the university and was a member of one of the historically Black fraternities, Alpha Alpha Alpha. Although supportive of building new fraternity and sorority houses in general, he is particularly interested in supporting his old Tri-Alpha chapter in their quest to build a new house.

Jackson decided to provide the resources to build an African-American fraternity house and is looking for suitable property on University land or in the alternative private property close to the university. He told Cogdell of his intentions and has already lobbied other board members to support his plan, of which he seems to have a strong level of support. Additionally, a number of his fellow Tri-Alpha alumni have pooled nearly $1 million to create an endowment at Cane Ridge to help defray the costs of hiring a resident director and university supported upkeep.

Like many southern universities, the campus of Cane Ridge is dotted with several Christian Student Centers that opened in the early days of the institution. These Christian student centers purchased property in the middle of the campus and are in varying degrees of prosperity. Trustee Jackson has focused on one particular Christian student center where he believes the African-American fraternity should be ideally located. The only stumbling block is that the property is owned by the Southern Baptist Conference and placing the fraternity on the property would require condemnation proceedings similar to the Beta Theta Nu fraternity.

The Baptist Student Center has languished in recent years and the property has also become an eyesore for the University and the community. The building housing the Baptist Student Center is in great need of renovation and it does not appear that the center has any resources to renovate its facility. The owner of the property, the Southern Baptist Conference headquartered in Atlanta, Georgia, has resources but prefers that its renter, the Center, pay for maintenance and upkeep. The Center rarely mows its grass or otherwise takes care of the property and the building seems to be falling apart and has become not only an eyesore but a potential fire trap for students who use the center.

Trustee Jackson believes that it is in the best interest

of all concerned to condemn the Baptist Student Center and build a new state-of-the-art Black fraternity on the property. He notes that in addition to helping to create a more "destination-like" campus, it is a great recognition of the 40% Black student enrollment. This, of course, will require condemnation proceedings and, even though it is likely that it will be controversial, Jackson wants to proceed immediately. His pledge to the fraternity is to build the fraternity house with no cost to anyone other than himself and has been willing to sign appropriate pledge documents to ensure the building of the house. Trustee Jackson has made his plans known widely and it is no secret to anyone that he will push hard for condemnation proceedings.

Let's Pause Again

1. Are the two condemnation processes similar? To what extent is one easier and one more difficult, and should Cogdell oppose or support either?
2. Do you see any hidden costs in allowing the fraternities to build their new houses? What responsibility and fiscal obligation does the university assume by allowing the construction to proceed?
3. Should the university be promoting the creation of 'secret' societies, especially student groups that are so strongly segregated? Is this made worse by the Beta's history of racial problems?
4. What are the public relations questions that will need to be pre-empted as the discussion moves forward about building the two fraternities? Are there opportunities present in these constructions projects that could add to the financial well-being of the institution?
5. Is Trustee Jackson using his influence inappropriately, not only as a trustee, but as a major benefactor? Is

there a need for institutional policy to govern both the expansion of Greek-life houses, but also the role of trustees in affairs such as these? Is this institutional policy, state policy, system policy?

The Beta house project proceeded with very few complications, as the owner of the body shop was not strenuously objecting to condemnation proceedings. He would have preferred to keep his property and working, but decided this was an easy way to sell-out his business and retire.

On the other hand, the Tri-Alpha fraternity that wants the University to condemn the Baptist Student Center is finding major objections from the Center's leadership who simply do not want to sell their property. Despite their lack of care of the Center, neither those working with the Center or the national office desires to leave the current location. They have indicated that they will sue the University and fight condemnation proceedings vigorously. Cogdell would like to support Trustee Jackson in his insistence to condemn the property, but he is very concerned about public outcry and opinion. After all, condemning a deteriorating body shop is one thing, but condemning a religious student center could be considered radically different. In addition to the notion of religion, the Baptist Student Center caters to an entirely White student population, and the idea of removing the property to place the Tri-Alphas there raises significant racial questions.

Cogdell informed the Chairman of the Board that he is not in favor of condemning the Baptist Student Center. He proceeds to lobby other members of the Board through personal, individual communication, but decides after the third phone call that it is a hopeless cause, most of the board has already given their promise to Jackson and they will support him in condemnation proceedings.

A Board meeting is scheduled for less than two weeks away, and both sides of the issue are lobbying hard to support their particular position. As might be expected, the entire issue becomes one of race and Jackson is making it clearly a race issue for everyone concerned. He has indicated to the media that if you condemn property for a White fraternity you should do the same for a Black fraternity. To do anything else would be racially insensitive and morally wrong, and the media is having a feeding frenzy with the issue. Additionally, the issue has divided the campus and caused much angst with the administration, Board of Trustees, alumni and students. Student protests on both sides of the issue have started and it appears that the whole matter has become emotionally charged. In fact, the Board meeting has the potential to become so antagonistic that Cogdell called in additional campus police to ensure order.

Ultimately the Board votes to back Jackson and approves condemnation proceedings against the Baptist Student Center. Hundreds of members of the Baptist church send letters of concern and objection to the Board and Cogdell. Many of the letters are mean spirited and even threatening. The Center and Baptist Conference immediately files a lawsuit against the Board and indicates that they will fight the proceedings every step of the way. It appears that the Board and Cogdell are in for a long fight, and whichever way they proceed someone will be extremely upset.

President Cogdell asks his Vice President for University Advancement to meet with Jackson and see if he can get him to slow down or back off for the good of the community and his university. The meeting does not go well and Jackson is insulted that Cogdell did not come himself, but instead, sent one of "his minions to do his bidding."

In the meantime, the unthinkable happens. Someone maliciously sets the Baptist Student Center ablaze. The fire destroyed the entire facility and it is a total loss but, but there are no fatalities or even serious injuries. The Baptist Convention was furious and accused the Black fraternity of torching their building. The fire marshal was certain the building had been destroyed deliberately but had no leads on the perpetrators.

A week later the Vice President for Advancement was walking over the remains of the burned out student center when an idea suddenly struck him. The university should immediately offer to buy the property and include in the purchase price similar acreage that the university owns several blocks to the north of campus. The property to be offered as a replacement is not adjacent to campus, but is within a short walking distance. In fact, it just might be possible to build a new Baptist Student Center with the cash given for the purchase of the lot. The Student Center would get cash and property in the purchase. On top of that, the Student Center had insurance that should cover furnishings and equipment. They just might get a new state of the art facility without any need to raise funds. They would only be giving up a few blocks further north from campus. Staying at the current location would not give them any cash to build a new building, which was sorely needed even before the fire.

The possible solution is proposed to Cogdell who sees the idea as a way to not only resolve the current problem, but very likely save his own job. He is not sure who to contact first, as his relationship with Jackson had deteriorated significantly since the entire ordeal had begun. He makes a quick decision to call his University legal counsel and get an opinion on the idea. He similarly calls an immediate meeting of his senior leadership team, thinking he has three things that need to happen: he needs the students and community to come together over the racially charged past couple of months, he needs the Student Center leaders to accept the land swap, and he needs Jackson to not fight the idea.

To Conclude the Discussion

1. Make a list of the possible advantages and disadvantages to the land-swap idea? Are there future problems that might come from creating this precedent?
2. What might Cogdell do to begin the healing process on a racially divided campus? Who should provide leadership to this process, and what kind of timeline and follow-up steps would be necessary?
3. What public relations strategy might be best structured to deal with the adversarial relationships on campus during the past several months? What long-term messaging might be developed to help prevent further racially-charged disruptions on campus, and who should be involved in creating and executing them?
4. What, if anything, can Cogdell do to work better with the Board, especially Jackson? Knowing that his term as chair will begin shortly, what would Cogdell's best strategy be?
5. How do Cogdell and the University's leadership team move forward with their plan for campus enrollment growth? How does enrollment planning move forward in light of the racially-charged tensions on campus? How do these past events impact planning for more Greek-life houses?

Case Study 13:
The Vanishing Name

Bradshaw College is a highly ranked national, private liberal arts college in the Pacific Northwest. Well respected nationally and considered to be one of the finest institutions of higher learning in the state, it enrolls around 1,300 students and is among the most nationally competitive institutions for admissions. Enrollment has remained steady for many years, and although the College could grow larger, the Board of Trustees has made a conscious decision to hold enrollment at a stable level and focus on the quality of the educational experience.

The College boasts an endowment of $375 million and a physical plant that is in top condition. Bradshaw College is one of the few liberal arts colleges of its class that has remained in excellent physical shape with beautiful facilities and an impressive physical plant. The leadership and Board take great pride in the idea that Bradshaw "looks like a college is supposed to look," and that nearly a dozen Hollywood movies have used its campus as a movie set.

With a national student body as well as a number of international students, the perception of the college is that if a student does not get into an Ivy League university, the student goes to Bradshaw. Some of the faculty have even called Bradshaw the "little-sister" of the Ivy League, a phrase that the President of the college does not like at all.

The President of Bradshaw College is 57 year old Dr. Astrid Markham. She has been at the college for 12 years and by all accounts has provided brilliant leadership. In addition to being a solid academic scholar, Markham is well respected for her fundraising abilities. During her tenure she has built new or renovated every academic facility on campus. She has an impressive list of accomplishments at the College and the Board of Trustees is hopeful that she will remain as president for many more years. She did her undergraduate work at Yale University and received her PhD from Stanford University. Her academic discipline is European history, and she is the author of numerous books and is a frequently requested keynote speaker. Her credentials, abilities, and reputation have been described as "beyond reproach." Before heading to the Pacific Northwest, she had been the provost and senior academic officer at Swarthmore College.

Markham has been able to obtain many multi-million dollar gifts for the endowment and physical plant during her tenure as president. She understands that development is a process and has put together a solid development office team that works alongside her. The Vice President for College Advancement is Mr. Terry Hartman and he has been with the college during the entire tenure of President Markham. Markham brought him to Bradshaw from Swarthmore where they worked together, and Hartman was the Vice President for Development. The two considered themselves to be very good friends and colleagues, and after working together for nearly 20 years, can almost anticipate what the other is thinking.

Hartman often considers Astrid a 'little-sister,' and is well past retirement age at 74. Again, Markham does not like the idea of "little-sister," but jokingly accepts the references from Terry as they work so well together. Hartman has told Astrid that he is willing to remain at the college for another 3 or 4 years, but that he wants to retire back to the East Coast where he and his family are all originally from. A few faculty members have expressed the opinion to the President and other senior officers that it is time for Hartman to consider retirement. They have noticed that he leaves the office early most days and can be found on the golf course or at the 19th Hole.

Markham actually approached her friend about this criticism she was hearing, and Terry became very defensive. "Astrid," he said, "in all the time we have worked together, have I ever, ever let you down? Have I ever failed to meet my goals? Have I failed to do something?" He also explained that he played golf as a way of cultivating prospects and almost all of his golf games were built around major donors. Markham was ashamed that she had questioned one of her most loyal friends and colleagues, apologized, but also reminded him that in this small college town "that people are watching you."

Hartman was not happy to hear what his "friend" said, and decided that he would continue to play golf as often as he liked. After all, he reasoned, "I have been responsible for building this college and raising millions of dollars and no one is going to tell me how to spend my time." In one of his golf games with two corporate executives, they began talking about Congressman Alexander Spencer.

Spencer is a prominent alumnus of the Political Science program of Bradshaw and a long serving United States Congressman from the district where Bradshaw is located. He is chairman of the powerful House Ways and Means Committee and is one of Bradshaw College's most successful alumni. While not considered to be a wealthy man himself, he has many wealthy admirers, associates and friends who have contributed generously to his campaign war chest for many, many years.

Several of the Congressman's friends first approached

Hartman and then President Markham about doing something substantial for Bradshaw College in the Congressman's name. The College has many prominent academic departments and two in particular are History and Political Science. Bradshaw, well known for both the social and hard sciences, has wanted a new facility for its social sciences that would include a large auditorium where prominent speakers could be heard. The cost of such a facility is projected to be over $10 million.

The alumni who want to honor the Congressman thought that they would be able to raise at least half this amount very quickly if done in honor of Congressman Spencer. President Markham was tasked with the responsibility to contact the Congressman and make him aware of this possibility and gain his endorsement. Markham debated sending Hartman in her place, as he was the first point of contact, but decided that she would take on the responsibility herself.

Before she left for Washington, she mentioned the progress on the gift idea to Hartman who said quietly, "Astrid, before you go, we need to have a conversation." He closed the door to her office with the hazy Pacific Northwest weather moving in. "So what do you know about Alex Spencer?" he started. He reported that there had been rumors for years that the Congressman was something of a 'playboy' while in DC. Markham, not knowing how honest Hartman was being after their confrontation over golf, decided to go ahead and leave for DC and keep her appointment. As she settled into her airplane seat, she decided to see what she could find out about "Playboy Congressman Alexander Spencer."

Let's Pause Here

1. What are your general thoughts on the idea of someone's friends raising money in someone else's name? Are your first impressions that this is a good idea? What complexities might arise from the use of this strategy?

2. Knowing that Vice President Hartman loves golf, and plays it quite a bit "for his job," is that or should that be a concern to the President? Was she right to confront him about it?

3. Should Markham be proceeding with her appointment with Congressman Spencer without doing a full-scale investigation as to whether there is any truth to his 'playboy' rumors?

4. With an estimated price of $10 million to construct some sort of new facility, what kinds of requirements should be put in place for fund raising gifts? Should the friends of the Congressman be required to raise the entire $10 million, or should the Bradshaw leaders be expecting them to raise something less, and use bonds to complete the construction?

5. Should there be any concerns about raising money and naming a building for a sitting elected official? What are the potential ramifications of political ideology, changing political votes and party control, etc., on naming an academic facility?

Markham found little online as she made her cross-country journey to meet the Congressman. They had met only once before, briefly, and she was warmly greeted. Spencer was visibly honored to be hosting his alma mater's president, an institution that he held very dear to his heart. Markham could feel the history of Congress and the political machine as she glanced at the pictures around the office of Spencer with US Presidents, Supreme Court justices, senators, etc. Spencer, considered one of the most powerful and connected people in Washington, had the pictures and connections to demonstrate his prominent role in American politics.

Markham explained to the Congressman that several of his close friends wanted to provide resources to build a social sciences building on campus. She further explained that they wanted the building to be named after him. These friends of the Congressman felt that they would be able to raise a minimum of $5 to $6 million to build the facility, and that the estimated the cost of the new building would be around $10 million. While it was possible to bond some of the building, Markham explained that she really hated to take on more debt at the college. She also took out one of the Admission Office's viewbooks, and showed the Congressman about where the building would be and that it would have the look and feel of the other red-brick, historic buildings.

Spencer was extremely excited by the news of his friends wanting to honor him. In fact he became quite emotional and it was obvious that he was quite touched. The Congressman immediately said that he thought he could find government resources to help complete the building. He said that he thought he could get some funds from the Defense Department having to do with leadership in international relations. The Congressman, thinking out loud, told Markham that "we may have to fudge a little in what we use the building for, but I can get you the $5 million to get this built."

Markham enjoyed the evening in Washington, having dinner with a very nice couple who had endowed a scholarship for needy students at Bradshaw. When she returned to her hotel, she was greeted by a bouquet of flowers with a kind note from Congressman Spencer, thanking her for her time and making the journey across the country.

Upon her return to campus, she had several email messages and telephone calls with various staff members in the Congressman's office, beginning the discussion of the "Congressman Alexander Spencer International Peace Center." She quickly began working on the Campus Master Plan to situate the new construction about where she had indicated in their conversation in Washington. There were few foundation issues or problems, and the Business Affairs staff were quick to draw up the initial blue-prints. They also prepared a bidding process to go out immediately, moving forward with construction immediately.

Markham was good at her job, and she called the Social Sciences faculty together, and over a light dinner, had a serious conversation about what would make the space unique and especially distinct to Bradshaw. She wrote down pages of ideas that she turned over to her Business Affairs staff and their eyes grew large as they saw the potential for creative uses of space. This building, cloaked in a historic shell, would be a state-of-the-art showcase building that would very likely win awards and receive national accolades.

Vice President Hartman was not intimately involved in this particular project, and that was somewhat unusual, but not unprecedented. There were some large gifts or pet projects that Markham took on herself that Terry simply supported. Sometimes gifts worked the other way, with development taking the lead and the President's office simply supporting the project. But as Terry heard more and more about the plans moving forward at a very rapid pace, he made an appointment to speak frankly with the President.

"Astrid, I think before you went out to meet the Congressman, I mentioned that there are rumors about Spencer, right?" he asked.

"You did, Terry," she responded, "But to be frank, I didn't find much and don't know if there is anything backing those rumors," she lied a bit, knowing that aside from one brief internet search, she had not looked very carefully at Congressman Spencer's personal life. "If it would help," she continued, "why don't you have your staff do a deep dig on him and see what you find out."

Hartman agreed to have his staff look around and see what they could find, but he also realized that as quickly as the President was moving, it was unlikely that he would be able to stop what he saw as a freight-train running down the track. She wanted the building. She wanted the gifts. She wanted what is best for Bradshaw.

Before Hartman can complete his task, Markham meets with the senior leadership of the development office and charges them with putting together a Blue Ribbon Task Force to raise money specifically for the Spencer building. Hartman felt put-off by Markham's speed and apparent dismissal of their agreement for him to do a "deep-dig" on the Congressman. The President wanted the Blue Ribbon Task Force up and running within two weeks, and she wanted to see significant results quickly.

Hartman followed Markham out of the meeting, stopping her in the hallway.

"Astrid, are you sure you want to do this? We're moving too fast. We need to really vet this thing before it goes forward another inch."

"Terry," she said as she looked at him coldly, "why don't you just go tee off and let us handle this one."

Let's Pause Again

1. What should Markham's reaction to the Congressman have been in response to his "fudge a little" comment? What kind of ethical concerns should Markham be thinking about?
2. Should Markham have spent more time making a decision about the possibility of the gift going forward, such as spending time researching the Congressman, discussing the building project with the Board, etc.? What would be her motivation for wanting to move so quickly?
3. Is Vice President Hartman spending too much time on the golf course, and should he have anticipated the request for a "deep-dig?" Should he have worked harder to control the situation as it began?
4. Tensions seem to be rising between the President and Vice President, with the President seeing the Vice President as a barrier to the gift and building moving forward. If you were witness to these conversations and the entire gift process, what would you do?
5. What responsibility does the Bradshaw team have for assuring that the alumni and friends of the Congressman fulfill their obligation? What kind of messaging would you recommend or would you envision to solicit gifts for a politician's recognition?

Hartman's thorough investigation into the Congressman turns up only what the media has reported, and some of those media outlets had been less than thorough in their own research. There were certainly rumors and tabloid reports of Congressman Spencer in bars and strips clubs, but no proof, no police reports, or confidential Congressional inquiries. Hartman was still cautious and thought that "where there is smoke, there is probably fire."

With some, but not much cause for concern, Markham began her efforts at raising the $5 to $6 million she was assured Bradshaw could for the building. Astrid and Terry appeared to be back on normal terms, although President Markham relied increasingly on the Associate Vice President for Development for her work with the project. Hartman was not overtly excluded, but he increasingly became an afterthought unless the conversation turned to golf.

After 18 months of fundraising progress the Blue Ribbon committee was at a standstill. Every prospect who had been identified had been cultivated and solicited, and the entire project had raised just under $3.5 million. No one in the Bradshaw database or on the prospect list that had been identified had the capacity for a six or seven figure gift. Two significant donors did say that they would make their gift after the building "breaks ground," and there was hope that they would be in the $1 million range, but that they would not make their pledge until then.

This information is communicated to Congressman Spencer by Markham, and although disappointed in the fundraising results, he is eager to have his name on a new facility and reports that he can "most likely" get the difference covered. Trusting in the Congressman's word, Markham convinces the Board to go ahead with a formal groundbreaking, hoping to rein in the additional prospects. A few of the Board members are concerned about starting the facility without all of the resources in hand, or at least firm pledges, as they had never tried anything like this before. The Chairman of the Board, along with Markham, convince the Board that moving forward is the best course of action, and that based on Spencer's comments, they will have cash in hand shortly and no debt. And, perhaps the most sophisticated building in the Northwest!

The Chairman of the Board practices due diligence and calls his old friend, the Congressman. Spencer allays any fears the Chairman has, and the Board votes 5-3 to approve the beginning of construction. This is the first split vote on any construction project that Hartman could ever remember, and he grows increasingly nervous.

On a warm March 1, ground is broken on the new social sciences building. The golden shovels were passed around and there was a great deal of joy as the Vice President of the United States offered a keynote address to the crowd about Congressman Spencer's record of service and commitment. Spencer delivered an evening lecture to a Political Science class, and to everyone's surprise, the Vice President dropped in un-announced to the class and joined the Congressman in a question-and-answer period with the students. The local, and even national media, covered the event, and the black-tie dinner was a huge success.

Hartman, committed and loyal to Markham and Bradshaw College, did not hesitate in his full and uncompromising support for the building and its importance. He did notice, however, at the end of the long dinner program that Spencer stumbled toward his waiting car and could not help but notice that he was not alone as he climbed into the black town car.

Markham felt reassured that she was making the right decision when even the Governor called her personally to congratulate her on the new facility and praise her for acknowledging the Congressman's commitment to the state. Despite the festivities, fundraising was still tepid and only an additional $550,000 was raised during these spring and summer months.

Construction was on target, and now $4 million raised

was being spent quickly as the facility began to take shape. The legislative session was about to start as Congress reassembled for the session in Washington, and hopes at Bradshaw for a quick allocation were rising. Markham knew that she needed the Congressman to come through with now $7 million. She did not hesitate at all when she picked up her cell phone with Terry's name flashing on the screen.

"Astrid," Hartman said, "turn on the tv immediately. Spencer's been arrested!"

The DC police were conducting their usual end-of-summer prostitution and drug raids, focusing on questionable strip-clubs and what were called "gentlemen's clubs." The DC police arrested nearly 30 people that evening, and did not recognize Congressman Spencer when they arrested him and took him to jail. He was charged with solicitation, public intoxication, possession of illegal drugs, and one count of conducting a lewd act in public. The Congressman's arrest was the lead story on each of the national news stations. There were immediate calls for the Congressman's resignation. An opposing party member began proceedings that afternoon to censure him and demanded his immediate resignation.

The Bradshaw Board called a special retreat for the coming weekend to discuss a "number of priorities for the College," yet everyone knew that it was in response to Spencer's arrest. All of the Board members were shocked about Spencer's arrest, and there was a great deal of speculation about whether he could "beat the charges." Hartman was quiet for the entire discussion, and he did not have to even give a report on the building's fundraising progress.

Within the week, two donors contacted President Markham asking for a refund of their gifts. They could not support, they noted, the behaviors of Congressman

Spencer. By the end of the second week following the arrest, 15 donors had asked for their gifts back, and in embarrassment, Congressman Spencer accepted a plea bargain for his behavior and resigned his congressional seat. There was no way any additional money would be coming for the completion of the building.

The Board began discussions of removing Spencer's name from what was now being referred to as the "proposed" building, and Markham was told that she needed to get to DC immediately to discuss the building with Spencer. She was also told that they would discuss her continuation as President when she returned.

To Conclude the Discussion

1. Who should bear ultimate responsibility for this entire situation? What should the consequences be for whomever is responsible? Would it be advisable to terminate President Markham over the building situation, and how would it help or hurt the institution?

2. What options does Bradshaw have at this point in time, with a partially completed building and a large debt to finish it? What message do they send to their alumni and other donors about the entire situation?

3. What obligation does the College have to the donors to the building? How do they communicate to them moving forward?

4. Draft a letter to donors to the building. What can you say to try and keep their gifts and encourage them to give more?

5. Should the College have engaged in construction when funding was not secure? Was there ever a guarantee that federal money would be available?

Case Study 14:
Internal Strife

St. Patrick's University is a private institution in the Washington, DC area, conveniently located on the Blue Metro Line. The University is well regarded nationally, and has a comprehensive curriculum including bachelors, masters and several doctoral programs, including one of the major History doctoral programs that focuses on Irish immigration. The Law School similarly has a strong national reputation, and it offers both a very traditional law school experience in addition to an "evening program" for those looking to attend on a part-time basis. The university will soon celebrate its 125th anniversary.

"St. Pat's" enrolls about 19,000 students from all over the United States, as well as a strong international enrollment. As a Catholic university, many students identify as Catholic, but nearly half of the enrollment comes from other denominations. The leaders of St. Patrick's work hard to market the institution as one that is open and encouraging of all faiths, and this is particularly true in its strong athletic programs. With teams in 16 men's and women's sports, the university boasts strong academic credentials for its student athletes. The Athletics Director has been at the institution for 35 years and is highly respected among alumni and the Board of Trustees. The athletics physical plant is in need of some long overdue refurbishment, particularly the outdoor fields and its aging basketball fieldhouse. The University participates in

NCAA Division I for most sports, but has a Division III football program.

The Board of Trustees of St. Patrick's is composed of business and professional leaders from all professions and walks of life, and in fact, the Chairperson of the Board is a member of the Evangelical Lutheran Church of America, an alumnus of St. Patrick's, and past president of the Alumni Association. And although the University has a strong, historical Catholic identity, less than half of the current board members are Catholic, and they have been at some odds with Catholic theology. This has brought some unwelcome negative publicity to the University, although comments by board members have not had an impact on enrollment. Comments by board members have, though, been somewhat controversial among the clergy and the dioceses that provide financial support for St. Patrick's.

The President of St. Patrick's is Dr. Chester Smithson, a layman, who is very well regarded in the DC area. He has only been at St. Patrick's for six months, and has taken over the institution after a long-serving President who was a priest. Smithson's appointment was supposed to represent a 'new reality' for the institution; one that is based on academic achievement and strong student enrollment, and less on theology and religious identification. Smithson has been able to counter, in a very short time, some of the negative publicity about the alignment of Catholic theology with academic freedom, and the faculty have seen him as a progressive, yet responsible, leader.

The past president had built the Board of Trustees as a strong fundraising group. They served on the Board not necessarily due to a belief or a 'calling,' but because they could help the University move forward both financially and in terms of strong business practices. One challenge that the Board has not been able to rectify is the relationship between the University's leaders, particularly those in the development office, and the SPU Alumni Association.

The SPU Alumni Association, also known as the "Order of the Shamrock" is an independent 501(c)(3) organization. With a separate Board of Directors, they operate independently of the University, although the staff of the association are, in fact, paid with university funds. The Alumni Association and the University have enjoyed a productive partnership for over 120 years, and the current rift is only several years old, coinciding somewhat with the previous president's change in thinking about the role of the Board of Trustees. In terms of structure, the Vice President for Development reports directly to President Smithson, but the Executive Director of the Alumni Association answers only to the SPU Alumni Association's Board of Directors, a common practice among colleges and universities.

The Alumni Association, through its membership dues and fundraising, is able to transfer cash to SPU to cover the salaries of its staff. This allows the Association's staff members to enjoy the benefits of being SPU employees, such as health insurance, retirement benefits, etc. The system has generally worked very well, but is predicated on rich information sharing between the Association and the SPU development office. When one office, for example, receives a change of address for an alumnus, the information would go into a centralized data base that is shared between the two offices. Despite the different offices and separate 501(c)(3) status, most alumni see no difference between the two offices or between the Association and the University; they simply see it all as St. Patrick's.

The Alumni Association hosts a wide range of stewardship events, ranging from pancake breakfasts to chili-feeds before basketball games. They have an active chapter system, mostly in the big cities along the East

Coast, many of which sponsor summer picnics and scholarship funds to send local high school students to SPU. They have also begun a number of travel and professional development programs for Association members, in addition to several affinity programs, such as life insurance discounts, special credit cards, and have even begun work on a retirement home complex for SPU graduates. On campus, they sponsor the SPU teaching awards and the massive homecoming week celebrations. In addition to their outreach, they also raise money for their activities from SPU alumni who are Association members, and although they do not actively seek endowment funds or large programmatic or academic gifts, they do have an annual fund that goes to support some of their activities.

Let's Pause Here

1. What potential conflicts do you see with the structure of the development office and the Alumni Association? Develop a list of advantages and disadvantages of this structure.
2. As a faith based institution, what observations would you have about a board of trustees that represents different faiths? What advantages or disadvantages would you see in such a composition?
3. A college president once observed that sports is the only way to increase the visibility of any higher education institution. How does a prominent athletic presence impact the university? How is this aligned with a mission of a faith-based university?
4. How does the institution change its mission in the eyes of alumni? Moving away from theology and its religious identification, what problems might the university anticipate?

5. Develop a series of strategy points to help the university introduce Smithson as a layman and new president. What concerns might alumni, students, faculty, and other stakeholders have with a lay-president? How can you use this change in leadership to benefit the institution?

The SPU Annual Fund, comprised of traditional direct mail pieces, telephone calls, and an online giving process raises money that the Association has a great deal of discretion over. Donors can, though, specify where their gift goes, and typically an alumnus will indicate an academic major, a particular scholarship fund, or "where the need is greatest." The category of greatest need is a general fund that the Association uses to promote SPU.

Gifts to the Association are receipted and then deposited in a different 501(c)(3) organization called the St. Patrick's University Foundation. That foundation is also independent of the University, has an independent Board of Directors, and serves as the "banker" and distributor of funds for foundation assets, which is basically all gift income. The Foundation receives gift income from the Development Office at SPU as well as the Association. So as gifts come into either of those offices, they are deposited with the Foundation, and then monthly, the Foundation pays out gift income to the University and the Association.

The Foundation has a number of regulations about how gifts are received and processed, and for the management of money, they do take a modest fee for their services of 50 basis points. The basis points model, which equates to one hundredth of one percent, allows the Foundation to charge based on the amount of money being managed, so the more money in their accounts, the more the Foundation gets to keep. This has been a point of contention for the

Alumni Association leadership, and on several occasions in the past, the Alumni Board considered breaking away from the Foundation and managing their own funds.

The annual fund has been moderately successful for many years under the Alumni Association's control and raises about $3 million per year. Approximately $1,750,000 of the annual fund comes designated by alumni to the Alumni Association, meaning that $1.25 million raised by the Association is "pumped back into the University" for programs, faculty, and student support. Only 14% of the SPU alumni make gifts to the Association, which is low compared to benchmark institutions and lower than the national average for similar private universities.

Because of this gift income the Alumni Association does not have a dues structure for membership. Any alumnus of the university is automatically a member of the Alumni Association and receives all of the benefits of membership. The leadership of the Alumni Association believes that this model works very well and benefits both the Association and academic programs on a continuing basis. Unlike the university foundation, the Alumni Association takes no fee or tax on gifts for administering the annual fund.

In addition to the Alumni Association, the Department of Intercollegiate Athletics collects money from alumni and friends of the university through an annual fund program. The Athletics program requires a contribution in order to purchase sporting event season tickets, when the Shamrocks are winning, especially in basketball, there is incredible demand for tickets. Athletics also sells premium suites for men's and women's basketball games, in addition to "preferred" parking options and private arena entry. With a Division III football program, there is not much emphasis on its success, and ticket sales are scarce. The football program is seen primarily as a student recruitment tool, where athletes are recruited and given academic scholarships, but the student choses SPU because of the chance to play football. The Athletics department raises an additional $5 million in annual gifts exclusively for athletics, and those gifts go into the Athletic Booster Foundation, another 501(c)(3) organization.

This SPU approach to the development structure of the Development office, the Alumni Association, Athletics, and the two foundations had worked relatively smoothly for the past 20-30 years. There were regularly disputes over some gift or who had the "rights" to a prospective donor, but these had been resolved through collaboration and open communication to the best that was possible. The senior group from each met on a regular basis with no clear authority figure among them, and with a strong level of mutual respect, they consistently "made the system work."

President Smithson had a significant fundraising background when he arrived at SPU, and believed the $35-40 million they raised each year was about half to a third of what they were capable of. He decided to change leadership in the senior development officer and hired a new Vice President for Development from another prominent Catholic institution in Boston. The President orchestrated a retirement of the previous Vice President, which proved to be not a very popular decision among alumni and friends of St. Patrick's. The previous Vice President had served SPU for over 20 years, and although he had reached retirement age, he did not want to retire and was essentially forced out.

Several members of the Board of Directors of the Alumni Association expressed their dismay at the retirement of the Vice President. They felt that the outgoing Vice President understood the importance of the collaborative relationship between the University and the Alumni Association and many of the Board members believed that the new Vice President would not have a similar appreciation for the organizational structure and independence of the Alumni Association. Rumors began on the first day of Samantha Dominguez's new appointment as Vice President that she did not like the annual fund arrangement and wanted to make a change immediately. The gossip intimated that the President did not like the arrangement either, and staff members throughout all of the development offices at SPU began to feel anxiety about possible changes even as Dominguez was just beginning her job.

Let's Pause Again

1. What advantages and disadvantages can you identify within the current structure for raising annual funds for St. Patrick's?
2. Identify several strategies that might be helpful for the Alumni Association to increase its level of participation with annual gifts. What strategies might be best targeted for young alumni? For mid-career alumni? For senior, retiring alumni?
3. How would you advise President Smithson to create oversight for the multiple-office approach to raising and managing money at SPU?
4. What opportunities for development do you see as possible with the arrival of Vice President Dominguez? Does SPU, as an institution, have a legal (or property) right to re-structure development however its leadership desires? Be sure to differentiate between 'right' and 'responsibility.'
5. Leadership transitions are always filled with rumors and gossip. If Smithson is interested in becoming

much more aggressive in development, what messaging might he create and use on campus to introduce the new direction and the new Vice President?

One of the first complaints Smithson heard when he became President was that the annual fund was not performing to its potential. All of the academic deans signed a memo to Smithson indicating that the annual fund was not helpful to their colleges, and that the money they received was minimal; they wanted change. He charged Dominguez with studying and devising a plan that would benefit academic fundraising and that included the annual fund as step in the fundraising ladder.

From the beginning of her tenure, Dominguez was skeptical of the Alumni Association's ability to handle the annual fund. She did not know of any other institution that had such an arrangement and believed that the annual fund should be under the purview of the development office, and she made her concerns known widely.

To further exacerbate relations with alumni personnel, during her first meeting of the development staff, Dominguez made a statement that she would later live to regret, saying "we've got so much work to do, so much potential, we need everybody fully committed to our efforts. If you want an easier job with less accountability go work in the Alumni office." She implied that fundraisers work much harder than friend-raisers in Alumni and before long her words were being quoted throughout the University. Her comments reached the Alumni Association staff within hours.

The Executive Director of the Alumni Association, Max Vivona, was furious when he heard about Dominguez's comments and immediately arranged an appointment to sound his objections. Vivona also made a personal appointment with President Smithson to inform him of the comments and voice his strenuous objections.

When Vivona arrived at the meeting with the President, he was shocked and surprised to find Vice President Dominguez in the President's office with the two of them. After exchanging pleasantries, reluctantly, the three got down to business with Vivona expressing disappointment and sincere dismay that his colleague would make such harsh statements about his alumni staff. He said that her comments had set back relations many years and had perhaps done irreparable harm to the two teams, and that Dominguez should issue a public apology to the Alumni staff.

President Smithson spoke up immediately and told Dominguez that he was disappointed in her comments and asked her to apologize to Vivona. Dominguez replied immediately that she believed her comments were taken out of context, that it was supposed to be only motivational, but that "if your skin is that thin, then I certainly do apologize."

The three sat silently for a moment, when Smithson then said, "the other reason I wanted to have you both here is that I've made a decision that you both need to know about." Smithson then indicated that he had decided to move all responsibility for the annual fund to the Development Office, effective immediately, and that control of all donor databases would also be the primary responsibility of the Development Office. His guiding rationale was that annual gifts, he believed, were introductions to giving at the University, and that there needed to be a structured approach to soliciting, monitoring, and growing donors.

Vivona was furious and objected strongly. Smithson would not be swayed and dismissed both with instructions that Dominguez should begin to draw up policy revisions immediately, and that the Alumni staff should be instructed to be helpful. "I don't want to hear about any lines in the sand or refusals to help," Smithson finished their conversation.

Vivona suspected collusion between Dominguez and Smithson, and even wondered if they had made the decision prior to her coming to campus. He immediately sent an email to his Board of Directors notifying them of the unilateral decision and asking the Board for ideas to respond with.

Dominguez similarly went to work looking at the existing infrastructure for soliciting annual gifts, everything from digital telephone calls to frequency of direct mail pieces. She began to identify space, and decided to conduct an external search for a Director of Annual Giving. She also called a meeting of the academic deans to identify how they could spend annual gift money, and made certain that all foundation annual fund accounts were established with dean's signature authority.

Vivona's email exploded with angry responses from the Alumni Board, highlighted by the fear that the Association's budget would be significantly hurt by the removal of the annual fund. Of the $1.75 million raised for the "greatest good," every penny was invested in the Association's work. Their budget would be cut in half with few options to recover that much money.

The Alumni Board spent a week developing, writing, and editing a strongly worded email to President Smithson and Vice President Dominguez. They believed that the University was moving away from its faith-based roots too quickly, that Smithson was interested only in "the bottom line," and Dominguez would bring ruin on the University. Smithson responded with a brief, one paragraph email indicating that the Association needed to move "into the

21st century" and that they should consider becoming a "dues based Association like every other university in America today."

The Association felt further insulted when it was realized that Athletics would be able to continue their own annual fund program. Staff in the Alumni office began looking for jobs, realizing that their potential for continued employment was suddenly in jeopardy, and, that none of them had been asked to join the new annual fund staff in Development. Vivona kept searching for options, maybe contacting the most influential donors, he thought?

On campus the new annual fund program was met with much enthusiasm. A new staff with a modernized aggressive approach nearly doubled the amount raised in the first year. The academic colleges were thrilled with the change and the resources they suddenly found that they had. Additionally, the major gifts staff members started to look at giving patterns with new enthusiasm and identified many large gift potential donors.

The Association lost multiple staff members and over 50% of their budget. Morale was poor, and Vivona continued to have a negative attitude. The Board supported him, but even they began to see that the University was moving on without the Association's endorsement. Vivona decided that the only option the Association had was to begin soliciting gifts in competition of the University, and to use those resources to support their own operations. The Board reluctantly agreed with Vivona, saying, "what other choice do we have?"

To Conclude the Discussion

1. Do you agree with President Smithson's decision to centralize the annual fund, moving it to the develop-

ment office? Could he have used a different message to achieve the same effect?

2. What reaction would you have had to Dominguez's comments about the alumni affairs staff? Do you agree with her comment?

3. What role do you believe a comprehensive alumni association should have? Describe what you perceive to be a best-practice for an alumni association to collaborate with a development office?

4. Depending upon your perception of the role of an alumni association, what functional responsibilities and expectations should be placed on an alumni association board? What outcomes or measures should be used to assess whether or not they are effectively meeting their goals?

5. Dominguez will ultimately be held responsible for all development activities associated with St. Patrick's. What approach should she take in working with the Alumni Association moving forward? How might she repair damaged relationships, and should she?

Case Study 15:
The Lost Merger

The year is 1975 and two prominent Midwestern colleges are located in the same small town of Decatur. Nestled along the Ohio River, the population of Decatur is 11,000 and the two colleges are the primary economic development provider for the entire region. The only other significant institution in the area is a state school for the blind which enrolls about 500 students. Enrollment in the school for the blind has been declining precipitously during the past 50 years when enrollment was well over 2,000 students. Decatur has a couple of small manufacturing plants, a tape factory and compressed lumber processing plant, that each employ under 100 people.

Holywell College is an all-women's institution of approximately 1,000 students. While its reputation is solid academically, it is perhaps best known as a finishing school for students from wealthy families. Students joke that the best degree at Holywell College is the "MRS." Faculty members and administrators of the college loath that expression and believe that it demeans the institution and its academic programs.

Perhaps the most pre-eminent program at Holywell is Equestrian Studies. One of the original programs at the college during its founding in 1875, students learn the skills of riding, horse, and stable management, and the college's stables and riding arenas are considered "world class." A number of national equestrian contests and competitions take place at Holywell College on a regular basis.

Holywell College is in reasonable financial condition and its enrollment has remained steady for the past 20 years, surviving the unrest felt on many single-gender colleges in the 1960s. As an all-women's college, the admissions staff has seen some decline in feeder high schools in the past few years. The college has a small endowment of only $15 million in spite of their best efforts to increase it through gift support. A recent capital campaign raised funds for the physical plant, but did not add measurably to the endowment. While the physical plant appears to be in good condition, many of the buildings are quite old and not based on steel frame structures, and the capital maintenance financing question looms heavily in the future.

The other college in Decatur is an all men's school, Western College. Founded by Methodists in the 1800's, when the mid-west was "the West:" Western is a well-respected liberal arts institution with 800 men enrolled. With a highly regarded pre-med and pre-law program, many students graduate and go on to law school or medical school. In fact, for many years Western College had an acceptance rate into medical school that approached 100%. Western is older than Holywell by about 50 years and was founded as a Methodist related institution. The college's tie to the United Methodist Church has diminished and it receives no support from the General Church Conference. There are a few small scholarships that were endowed by local churches but these provide nominal support to the college and it students.

Western students generally believe that their institution is better than Holywell and even joke about the academic discipline at their "sister" institution. However, the colleges entered into an agreement many years ago that allows students to take general education courses that count toward their degrees at either institution. Many of the men take courses at Holywell because they believe them to be easier, but few women take courses at Western because they believe the courses to be harder, although there may be other reasons, such as women feeling uncomfortable going to Western alone to take classes with all men.

Western has been experiencing a rather dramatic enrollment decline for about the past decade. Some believe that the admissions requirements are too rigorous and exceptional students who are accepted to Western typically choose another institution of greater prominence, such as Grinnell, Macalester, and Oberlin. As one student put it "why would I go to Western if I can go someplace that people have actually heard of?" Understandably the faculty have been very reluctant to change the admission requirements, and it has become a source of conflict between the administration and the faculty. The faculty, and actually many of the Trustees, want to keep the requirements at the highest possible level, and the administration believes that minor softening of entrance requirements would boost enrollment considerably; an ongoing debate with no resolution in sight.

Western has been able to pay its bills and is in fair financial condition, but like Holywell, it has a very small endowment. The size of the endowment has plagued Western's history despite best efforts to raise private funds. The current size of the endowment is approximately $35 million, about one-tenth of its competitors, and it provides little operating revenue to assist with investing in college resources.

Western generally lives a "hand to mouth" existence and spends every penny of tuition and gift income that it receives, but despite this, has been able to keep its physical plant in good condition. Most of the buildings are steel structures and the college has a beautiful campus aesthetically. Parents and students are extremely impressed by the beautiful quad at the center of campus when they visit and the institution has the appearance of being a thriving, well-off college.

The President of Western is Dr. Benjamin Rust, a year into his job. He realizes the financial state of the college, and estimates that enrollment needs to increase to at least 1,000 students, or Western will not be open in the long term. He begins to offer "scholarships" in the form of tuition discounts to help grow enrollment. And with full Board support, he plans to double the endowment in the next five years.

The President of Holywell has been at the helm of the institution for 15 years and is highly respected. Dr. Joyce Caldwell believes strongly in the importance of women's colleges and is known nationally as a proponent of women's education. She has made public statements that Holywell College will forever remain a women's institution. And although she recognizes the need for increased revenue to update the campus, she did not realize just how cash-poor the institution was until a small fire destroyed a floor of a residence hall. The college had to shutter the building for the remainder of the academic year rather than make costly repairs to re-open it.

Let's Pause Here

1. If you were hired as fundraising consultant for Holywell and for Western, how would you go about setting priorities for their development goals?
2. Based on what you know about these two institutions, what strategies might you development to increase fundraising success? What about alumni engagement?

3. From a strategic perspective, how might these two colleges collaborate to better assure a sound financial future? What leadership would need to be necessary to make your ideas happen?
4. Facilities can be difficult to raise funds for, especially when they are repairs to facilities rather than new construction. Identify what might motivate a donor to make a contribution to building renovation. How could either institution appeal to the motivation you identify?
5. Tuition discounting refers to the practice of reducing what a student would pay in order to get the student to enroll, with the thinking that some partial payment is better than none. How could this type of tuition pricing practice help or hurt an institution over a long period of time?

Separating Western and Holywell physically was "The Run," which was actually a half-mile strip of lower-income housing and old small houses. The brick street had old, large oak trees and a distinguished history of its working-class roots. Currently, though, the strip was notorious for crime and few students walked the strip after dark, hence students referred to the area as a place to "*run*" through.

As Rust works to secure a strong financial future for Western, he begins to explore the idea of becoming co-educational. This would round out his planning, along with tuition discounts and endowment growth. He held a confidential discussion with the Western Board in an effort to convince them that all men's colleges are not sustainable in the future. Nationally the number of all male colleges has declined over the past several years and many prominent all-male institutions have made the leap to coeducation. He believes that the college must make this change soon or suffer continued enrollment decline. The younger Trustees see value in the co-education plan, but the majority, all older Trustees, stand in strong opposition.

The chairman of the Western Board of Trustees is an alumnus of the class of '48 and is a prominent business executive. He owns a large manufacturing plant several hours to the north, and his family is quite wealthy. Mr. James Cornelius Spoon has been very generous with his time to the College, although he has not made any significant cash contributions. Spoon Residence Hall on the Western campus was given to the College by his late mother. Spoon has educated two of his three sons at Western College and believes it to be one of the finest institutions in the Midwest. As chairman of the Board of Trustees he is determined to do all he can to secure the financial future of the institution while he is Board chairman, and he intends to use his own wealth to that end.

The chairwoman of the Board of Trustees of Holywell College is Dr. Madeline Johnson who is a surgeon in a large city several hours away. She fully supports President Caldwell in the desire to remain a women's institution. Dr. Johnson is well known throughout the state for supporting women's causes and believes that women in general have not enjoyed the same educational benefits as men. She is not a graduate of Holywell College, however, her daughter is a graduate.

At a small private dinner among the President and Board of Western, Chairman Spoon opened the discussion about the future of the college. The discussion included conversation about coeducation and increasing the student body. One of the trustees made the comment "why don't we just merge with Holywell rather than go coed? " His argument was that to go coed would be in direct competition of the sister institution only blocks away. This might cause them to convert to coeducation and launch an "admissions war" that no one would ultimately win. "In fact, given the lower admissions requirement of Holywell, they just might be able to out maneuver us!"

Spoon had not thought of a merger and quickly moved the discussion to one about getting the two colleges together. They talked about merging physical plants, reducing costs for general education core instruction, and even combining endowments. Spoon asked Rust his opinion, to which he responded "I rather doubt that the Holywell people would have an interest. They are all very pro-women, and I don't think they would like the idea of joining forces." Rust actually had no idea what the Holywell Board or administration might think of such a merger, and was able to end the evening's conversations with no commitment of action.

A month later, Chairman Spoon called Rust and told him he wanted to come visit him at the college and have a private meeting about the institution's future. He said the meeting was of utmost importance and he only wanted the two of them to meet.

Spoon arrived at the president's office early and was immediately ushered in to see President Rust. Spoon told the President that he had been giving a great deal of thought to the future of the college, and that he believed that it was his destiny to secure the college for the future while he was chairman of the board. He then announced that he and his family had met and made a monumental decision with the best interests of the college in mind.

Spoon then announced that "we have decided to dissolve the family foundation and give the entire proceeds to Western."

Rust was thrilled with this news and got up from his

chair to embrace Spoon. As he crossed the desk, Spoon went on to say that the $140 million he was willing to transfer is predicated on Western and Holywell merging. Spoon said that he was convinced that a merger was in the best interest of all involved and that remaining an all-male institution was simply not sustainable in the modern world. Spoon also commented that he "did not favor going coed and angering countless Holywell College alumni as well as the administration, board members and others. Too many of our alumni are married to Holywell women and trying to compete directly with them for female students would be "unfortunate and hurtful."

Rust begged Spoon to help Western go co-educational rather than merge, but Spoon would not budge on his mandate. He asked for a meeting of the full Board, combined with the leadership of Holywell. Rust convinced Spoon to let him meet individually with the Holywell Board, and he did so keeping it a secret from President Caldwell, claiming "she'll just say no to the whole thing without even thinking about it!"

Spoon placed a private call to Holywell Board Chair Johnson, asking for a confidential meeting. Johnson agreed without knowing what Spoon had planned, but he made additional calls to the majority of the Holywell Board without permission or their knowledge of what these individual meetings were for.

Let's Pause Again

1. Was it an appropriate action by Spoon to make such a request as merging colleges as a requirement for his contribution? If so, how should he have handled making such a gift? If not, where does an institution 'draw the line' in accepting a contribution for a requested action?

2. Was President Rust's behavior appropriate? How does he balance the need for financial stability and satisfying a donor with the knowledge that Caldwell would not agree to merging the institutions? Was operating in secrecy his only option?
3. Recognizing the challenges of an all-male or all-female college, and using historical precedence for these types of institutions, what strategic thinking should the college leaders be considering at this time? How do they effectively involve the development and college relations staff?
4. Where are the alumni in these discussions of the college's future? Should both sets of college leaders be more aggressive in their fundraising efforts?
5. Where do both Rust and Caldwell prioritize their campus planning needs? How should these needs be aligned with development objectives?

Western had a Spring board meeting planned, and it so happened that the Holywell board was meeting on the same weekend. Rust was working against the deadline of these meetings and wanted to create a merger plan, and consensus, by the time the two boards met.

Rust's first call on the matter to Caldwell was an invitation to dinner for the Holywell Board Executive Committee, to dine with the Western Board Executive Committee. Caldwell knew nothing of the merger talks, and agreed thinking it was a polite gesture and an act of kindness for two colleges with similar problems.

The Western Board had been briefed on the $140 million gift and merger plans, and as the two Executive Committees sat down, the Holywell leadership was stunned by what came out of Rust's mouth.

"The reason we've invited you to dinner here tonight

is to formally request and put before the Holywell Board a plan to merge our two colleges," Rust began. "We have secured an outright cash gift of $140 million to be placed into an endowment for our two colleges, provided that we merge."

Caldwell was speechless, and her stunned silence turned to anger as two of her own Executive Committee members began to extoll the virtues of merging. Rust had not been able to gain the full support of the Holywell Executive Committee, and the dinner party turned into a tense discussion with several Holywell Trustees leaving without having anything to eat.

As the Western Board members looked curiously at each other following the tense conversation, their consensus statement was "women!"

Rust had a local attorney work with his in-house legal counsel to draft a resolution to merge the two institutions. Based on the somewhat positive "let's discuss it" attitude that he had received from Holywell Chair Johnson, he had copies of the resolution sent to her hotel room late that evening with a note asking her to discuss it, and vote if appropriate, on the resolution at their board meeting the next day.

Johnson did introduce the resolution and briefed the Holywell board on the $140 million gift, an assurance of a stable future. The board debated what had become known as the "Silver Spoon plan," and ultimately it was voted down by a 22-13 margin. Caldwell, who did in fact favor the idea of maintaining Holywell as an all-women's college also realized that such an idea would be difficult in the future. She had admitted as much to the Board, but more importantly derided Rust and the Western leadership for their secretive behaviors. The Board also voted to support an elimination of any general education course exchange between the two institutions.

Johnson, the Holywell Board Chair, resigned shortly after the meeting. Having clandestine discussions with Rust was inappropriate, she said in her resignation letter. She also applauded Caldwell for "sticking to her guns" and taking a chance on what she personally believed in.

Spoon, angry over the outcome of the dinner meeting and subsequent Holywell rejection of the proposal, told Rust that he was withdrawing his $140 million gift and immediately resigned as Chairman of the Board. The merger was dead, and support from the Spoon family became nonexistent.

Over the course of many years, other attempts at merger were made but to no avail. Relations between the two colleges had become distant, with Rust and Caldwell remembering all too well the "near merger" as Rust referred to it, or the "hostile takeover bid," as Caldwell called it. In 1985 Western College became a co-educational institution, and shortly thereafter, Holywell College did the same. An "admissions war" began to some extent, as area high schools were flooded with competitive scholarship offers and tuition discounts. Coeducation enrollment temporarily revived Western, as their enrollment grew to 950 students. However the endowments of both colleges remained quite small and meeting annual budgets became much more difficult. In 1999 Holywell College decided to launch a considerable online degree program in academic areas that they currently offered, and the effort proved to be extraordinarily successful. Caldwell, and her successor, structured the online programs to provide the much needed cash to protect the base or "core" operation of the liberal arts experience at Holywell, including facility renovation. Additionally, the online program cash allowed

Holywell to expand its equestrian program to the extent that its national reputation brought in significant continuing education revenues. Caldwell was quick to share the credit for the renaissance and reinvention of Holywell, and was able to hand-pick her successor.

Western College, on the other hand, continued on the same path as they had for 150 years but did make several attempts to introduce new academic programs that would appeal to more students. The traditional humanities based programs struggled for enrollment, as they did in all of higher education, and the stringent admissions requirements similarly limited the number of students who considered Western. Enrollment for the college dropped to 700 students by 2005 when Rust retired. By 2012, Western was in financial distress and began to sell its assets, including property holdings. In 2017, the college was unable to fund its payroll and began closure proceedings.

In the early-2000's, Holywell also invested heavily in an external consulting company to assist with fundraising activities. With some available cash, they were able to purchase a donor database and to make use of a private company to help identify alumni of wealth. In 2002 the College was aggressively raising money from alumni, corporations, and foundations, and by 2017, Holywell's endowment approached $75 million and its future seemed well assured.

To Conclude the Discussion

1. How important is institutional leadership in aligning goals and resources? To what do you attribute Western's long-term inability to grow resources?
2. Were you surprised by Spoon's resignation from the Board? Was this a reflection of him not getting his way,

or was he discouraged by Rust's leadership ability? Might there have been another motive for his desire to make a $140 million gift?

3. Might the outcome of the attempted merger, and in fact the legacy of both institutions, have been different had Rust involved Caldwell openly from the beginning? Should both full boards have been involved in merger discussions from the time of Spoon announcing his plan?

4. Outline what you think might be a good structure for discussing an institutional merger. How long do you perceive that it should take for a smooth transition of institutional mergers?

5. Holywell seemed to be pursuing a system of revenue diversification, and it seemed to work. How would you characterize the activities of Western? What factors might have led to their ultimate demise?

Suggested Fund Raising Readings

Over the past several decades, there has been a significant amount of research and writing about fundraising, both in higher education and in other non-profit sectors. The writings have been disseminated broadly in practitioner and trade publications, in refereed academic journals, and even newspapers and popular media. The study of fundraising has been particularly popular in academic dissertation writing, perhaps a function of the number of fundraising practitioners who continue their education by earning advanced academic degrees. This bibliography was constructed from the readings that helped to inform the case studies included in this book.

Anderson, S. (2003). *Fundraising programs in community colleges: Factors that contribute to effectiveness.* Doctoral dissertation, Texas A&M University at Commerce.

Bass, D. (2009). College fundraising: Is there a new normal? *Trusteeship, 17*(6), 8-12.

Bruggink, T., & Kamran, S. (1995). An econometric model of alumni giving: A case study for a liberal arts college. *The American Economist, 39*(2), 53-60.

Borden, V. M. H., Shaker, G. G., & Kienker, B. L. (2014). The impact of alumni status on institutional giving by faculty and staff. *Research in Higher Education, 55*(2), 196-217.

Caboni, T. C. (2010). The normative structure of college and university fundraising behaviors. *Journal of Higher Education, 81*(3), 339-365.

Castaneda, M. A., Green, J., & Thornton, J. (2008). Competition, contractibility, and the market for donors to nonprofits. *Journal of Law, Economics, and Organization, 24*(1), 215-246.

Cheslock, J. J., & Gianneschi, M. (2008). Replacing state appropriations with alternative revenue sources: The case of voluntary support. *Journal of Higher Education, 79*(2), 208-229.

Chung-Hoon, T. L., Hite, J. M., & Hite, Steven, J. (2007). Organizational integration strategies for promoting enduring donor relations in higher education: The value of building inner circle network relationships. *International Journal of Educational Advancement, 7*(1), 2-19.

Clotfelter, C. (2003). Alumni giving to elite private colleges and universities. *Economics of Education Review, 22*(2), 109-120.

Cohu, J. (2012). *Factors influencing fundraising success in church-related colleges and universities*. Doctoral dissertation, Eastern Michigan University, Ypsilanti.

Comegno, M. H. (2004). *Fundraising effectiveness: Definition and measurement at a women's college*. Doctoral dissertation, University of Pennsylvania, Philadelphia.

Cook, W. B. (1997). Fund raising and the college presidency in an era of uncertainty: From 1975 to present. *Journal of Higher Education, 68*(1), 53-86.

Cunningham, B., & Carlena, C. F. (2002). The determinants of donative revenue flows from alumni of higher education: An empirical inquiry. *The Journal of Human Resources, 37*(3), 540-569.

Curry, J., Rodin, S., & Carlson, N. (2012). Fundraising in difficult economic times: Best practices. *Christian Higher Education, 11*(4), 241-252.

Daly, S. (2013). Philanthropy, the new professionals and higher education: The advent of directors of development and alumni relations. *Journal of Higher Education Policy and Management, 35*(1), 21-33.

Davis, S. R. (2013). *A portraiture of nonprofit leadership in educational fundraising*. Doctoral dissertation, University of Nebraska-Lincoln.

Doty, D. G. (2007). *Institutional strengths, fundraising messages, and private giving outcomes in Tier One Research Universities*. Doctoral dissertation, University of Nebraska-Lincoln.

Drezner, N. D. (2013). The Black church and millennial philanthropy: Influences on college student prosocial behaviors at a church-affiliated Black college. *Christian Higher Education, 12*(5), 363-382.

Durango-Cohen, E., & Balasubramanian, S. (2015). Effective segmentation of university alumni: Mining contribution data with finite-mixture models. *Research in Higher Education, 56*(1), 78-104.

Edgington, K. D. (2013*). Leadership in higher education fundraising: Chief fundraiser style and follower self-efficacy*. Doctoral dissertation, University of Texas at Dallas.

Eversden, G. K. (2003). *Characteristics of selected fundraising programs: Case studies of two Carnegie I Research-Extensive universities.* Doctoral dissertation, Southern Illinois University at Carbondale.

Gearhart, G. D. (2005). *Philanthropy, fund raising, and the American capital campaign: A practical guide.* Washington, DC: NACUBO.

Goddard, C. (2009). *Presidential fundraising colleges in the Midwest: A case study.* Doctoral dissertation, University of Nebraska-Lincoln.

Harrison, W. B., Mitchell, S. K., & Peterson, S. P. (1995). Alumni donations and colleges' development expenditures: Does spending matter? *American Journal of Economics and Sociology, 54*(4), 397-412.

Herley, W. T. (2012). *Public higher education fundraising: Selected Florida university leaders' perceptions of influence on larger gifts.* Doctoral dissertation, University of South Dakota.

Hillman, J. (2002). *An investigation of the current status of fundraising activities and training within student affairs divisions in Texas colleges and universities.* Doctoral dissertation, University of North Texas.

Holmes, J., Mediz, J., & Sommers, P. (2008). Athletics and alumni giving: Evidence from a highly selective liberal arts college. *Journal of Sports Economics, 9*(5), 538-552.

Holquist, G. W. (2011). *Identifying key determinants that influence athletic alumni intent to give financially to intercollegiate athletic department fundraising campaigns.* Doctoral dissertation, University of Minnesota.

Hunsaker, J. S. (2010). Fundraising and values: When do you say 'no' to money. *Journal of Cases in Educational Leadership, 13*(1), 48-60.

Kimball, B. A. (2014). The first campaign and the paradoxical transformation of fundraising in American higher education, 1915-1925. *Teachers College Record, 116*(7), 1-44.

Lindahl, W., & Winship, S. (1992). Predictive models for annual fundraising and major gift fundraising. *Nonprofit Management Leadership, 3*(1), 3-64.

Marr, K., Mullin, C., & Siegfried, J. (2005). Undergraduate financial aid and subsequent alumni giving behavior. *The Quarterly Review of Economic and Finance, 45*(1), 123-143.

McAllister, S. M. (2013). Toward a dialogic theory of fundraising. *Community College Journal of Research and Practice, 37*(4), 262-277.

Miller, M. T. (1993). Historical perspectives on the development of academic fund raising. *Journal of Instructional Psychology, 20*(3), 237-242.

Monks, J. (2003). Patters of giving to one's alma mater among young graduates from selective institutions. *Economics of Education Review, 22*(2), 121-130.

Nehls, K. (2012). Leadership transitions during fundraising campaigns. *Innovative Higher Education, 37*(2), 89-103.

Okunade, A. A. (1996). Graduate school alumni donations to academic funds: Micro-data evidence. *American Journal of Economics and Sociology, 55*(2), 213-229.

Okunade, A., Wunnava, P., & Walsh, R., Jr. (1994). Charitable giving of alumni: Micro-data evidence from a large public university. *American Journal of Economics and Sociology, 53*(1), 73-84.

Overley, K. S. (2006). *Public university leaders as fundraisers.* Doctoral dissertation, University of Texas at El Paso.

Pinchback, G. K. (2011). *Fundraising and community college chief executives: A study of development in the Southern Regionall Education Board states.* Doctoral dissertation, Arkansas State University.

Pottick, K. J., Giordano, S., & Chirico, D. E. (2015). Creating a culture of student philanthropy to address financial challenges in universities. *Journal of Social Work Education, 51*(2), 207-221.

Rau, N. (2014). *Predictive modeling of alumni donors: An engagement model for fundraising in postsecondary education.* Doctoral dissertation, James Madison University.

Satterwhite, C. R. (2004). *The function of university presidents and CEO's in fundraising: A study of public universities with capital campaigns less than $100 million.* Doctoral dissertation, Texas Tech University.

Satterwhite, C. R., & Cedja, B. (2005). Higher education fund raising: What is the president to do? *International Journal of Educational Advancement, 5*(4), 333-342.

Sazonov, S., Kharlamova, E., Chekhovskaya, I., & Polyanskaya, E. (2017). Mechanism of determination of effectiveness of spending assets on endowment funds on the basis of mathematical models. *International Journal of Education Management, 31*(1), 21-29.

Schanz, J. M. (2012). *Differences in university fund raising: The role of university practices and organization.* Doctoral dissertation, State University of New York at Albany.

Stinson, J. L., & Howard, D. R. (2010). Intercollegiate athletics as an institutional fundraising tool: An exploratory donor-based view. *Journal of Nonprofit and Public Sector Marketing, 22*(4), 312-335.

Sturgis, R. (2006). Presidential leadership in institutional advancement: From the perspective of the president and vice president of institutional advancement. *International Journal of Educational Advancement, 6*(3), 221-231.

Thorley, W., Majoribanks, B., & Kranz, J. (2014). Enhancing the undergraduate student experience via fund-raising partnerships: An action research project. *Educational Action Research, 22*(4), 552-567.

Wagoner, R. L., & Besikof, R. J. (2011). Community college fundraising: The voluntary support of education survey as a sampling tool for research. *Community College Journal of Research and Practice, 35*(1/2), 74-87.

Weerts, D. J., Cabrera, A. F., & Sanford, T. (2010). Beyond giving: Political advocacy and volunteer behaviors of public university alumni. *Research in Higher Education, 51*(4), 346-365.

Weerts, D. J., & Ronca, J. M. (2009). Using classification trees to predict alumni giving for higher education. *Education Economics, 17*(1), 95-122.

Wesley, D. M. (2007). *Catholic college and university presidents: Fundraising initiatives and identity maintenance.* Doctoral dissertation, Johnson and Wales University.

Whitaker, S. D. (2005). *The role of the private college president in fundraising: A comparative case study.* Doctoral dissertation, University of Louisville.

Willemain, T. R., Goyal, A., Van Deven, M., & Thukral, I. S. (1994). Alumni giving: The influences of reunion, class, and year. *Research in Higher Educaiton, 35*(5), 609-629.

Wood, J. S. (2012). *Rural community college fundraising: A multi-site case study exploring the characteristics and motivations of alumni supporters.* Doctoral dissertation, Oregon State University.

Wu, K., & Brown, M. (2010). An examination of persistence in charitable giving to education through the 2002 economic downturn. *International Journal of Education Advancement, 9*(4), 196-219.

Wunnava, P., & Lauze, M. (2001). Alumni giving at a small liberal arts college: Evidence from consistent and occasional donors. *Economics and Education Review, 20*(6), 553-543.

Yi, D. T. (2010). Determinants of fundraising efficiency of nonprofit organizations: Evidence from US public charitable organizations. *Managerial and Decision Economics, 31*(7), 465-475.

About the Authors

Dr. G. David Gearhart is Chancellor Emeritus and Professor of Higher Education at the University of Arkansas. Previously he served as Vice Chancellor for University Advancement at the University. He was Senior Vice President and Managing Director of the international consulting firm Grenzebach, Glier & Associates, Inc. Before his service at GG&A, Gearhart was Senior Vice President for Development at Penn State University, during which time he was named a Fulbright Scholar, studying at Oxford University. Early in his career he served as Vice President for Development at Hendrix College in Arkansas and Director of Development at Westminster College. His Bachelor of Arts degree is from Westminster College where he was named a distinguished alumnus in 1992. Both his law degree and his Doctor of Education degree are from the University of Arkansas. He is the author of two books on fundraising and numerous articles. He and his wife Jane have two children and five grandchildren.

Dr. Michael T. Miller is Dean of the College of Education and Health Professions at the University of Arkansas where he is also a Professor of Higher Education and holder of the Henry Hotz Endowed Chair. Miller has served as Associate Dean of the College of Education at San Jose State University, Chair of the Higher Education Program at the University of Alabama, and Director of Annual Giving at the Southern Illinois University Foundation. He has served as president of two national associations, has served as the editor of three different academic journals, has published nearly 300 articles and book chapters, has authored five and edited eight books. He has also chaired nearly 100 doctoral dissertations and has authored over $3.5 million in externally funded grants. He holds a bachelors degree in Political Science and masters degree in Higher Education from Southern Illinois University and a Doctorate of Education from the Teachers College at the University of Nebraska. He and his wife, Lara, have three children.

Made in the USA
Lexington, KY
08 February 2018